Policies for
APPRENTICESHIP

ORGANISATION FOR ECONOMIC CO-OPERATION AND DEVELOPMENT

The Organisation for Economic Co-operation and Development (OECD) was set up under a Convention signed in Paris on 14th December 1960, which provides that the OECD shall promote policies designed:
- to achieve the highest sustainable economic growth and employment and a rising standard of living in Member countries, while maintaining financial stability, and thus to contribute to the development of the world economy;
- to contribute to sound economic expansion in Member as well as non-member countries in the process of economic development;
- to contribute to the expansion of world trade on a multilateral, non-discriminatory basis in accordance with international obligations.

The Members of OECD are Australia, Austria, Belgium, Canada, Denmark, Finland, France, the Federal Republic of Germany, Greece, Iceland, Ireland, Italy, Japan, Luxembourg, the Netherlands, New Zealand, Norway, Portugal, Spain, Sweden, Switzerland, Turkey, the United Kingdom and the United States.

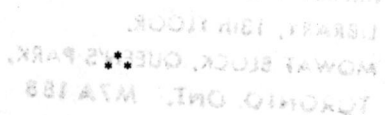

© OECD, 1979
Queries concerning permissions or translation rights should be addressed to:
Director of Information, OECD
2, rue André-Pascal, 75775 PARIS CEDEX 16, France.

CONTENTS

Preface 5

Summary and Main Conclusions 7

I. Introduction 23

II. Main Features of Apprenticeship 28

    A. Legal Framework and Administrative Structure 28

        1. Legislative Provisions 28
        2. Administrative Structures 29

    B. Number and Type of Apprenticeable Occupations 31

    C. Admission to Apprenticeship 33

        1. Age of Entry and Completion 33
        2. Standards of Entry 34
        3. Limits to Recruitment 35
        4. Termination before Completion 37
        5. Admission of Special Groups 38
        6. Employment after Apprenticeship 41

    D. The Structure and Content of Training 42

    E. Examination and Certification 46

    F. Financing of Apprenticeship 50

        1. Employer Responsibility 50
            a) How many employers train apprentices? 50
            b) Training costs 53
            c) Conjunctural and secular influences on intake 56
        2. Collective Financing 59
        3. Government Financial Assistance to Employers .. 63
        4. Public Financial Aid to Apprentices 67

III. Chief Developments in Apprenticeship in Recent Years 69

    i) Internal Features 70
    ii) Relationship to Education 74
    iii) Relation to Other Skill Training 75

IV. Issues and Policy Implications 77

    Criticisms of Apprenticeship 77
    Other Issues 80

References 83

Appendix: Statistical Tables 89

PREFACE

The main purpose of this report, which has been prepared under the work programme of the OECD Education Committee in collaboration with the Manpower and Social Affairs Committee, is to analyse current trends and issues in apprenticeship and in policies for apprenticeship in Member countries in a way that may be informative and useful to governments in considering this and alternative forms of skill training. The report is limited to those OECD countries in which apprenticeship is an established means of providing skill training, whether it is the dominant form or secondary to other methods. It excludes countries where apprenticeship exists on a very small scale only.

The report is based on information provided to the Organisation by the authorities in Member countries, on public sources and on visits to some of the countries concerned by Dr. Beatrice G. Reubens, Senior Research Associate in Conservation of Human Resources, Columbia University, New York, who, in her capacity as consultant to the Organisation, is also the principal author of the report.

The present text has been revised to take account of suggestions made by members of the Education and the Manpower and Social Affairs Committees and the authorities in the Member countries. An earlier version was made available as background reference material to the High Level Conference on Youth Unemployment held by the Organisation in December 1977.

This report is published under the responsibility of the Secretary-General.

SUMMARY AND MAIN CONCLUSIONS

THE GENERAL CONTEXT

There is at present considerable interest in apprenticeship in a number of OECD countries for two main reasons. It has different, and at times conflicting, roles for the individual, the enterprise and the economy. Moreover, long-term trends and conjunctural variations in the economy make the future of apprenticeship uncertain.

For the individual, apprenticeship is a means of easing the transition from school to working life and introducing young people to adult roles and responsibilities in employment; a method of long-term skill training which combines instruction and practical experience; and a way of continuing part-time general education. It is sometimes an alternative route to higher education and an avenue of access to skilled occupations for disadvantaged and handicapped young people. For employers, apprenticeship is a source of manpower in the short term, a means of providing its future skilled personnel and of adapting the skills of the personnel to changes in production, markets and technology in the enterprise. For the economy, apprenticeship is a means of replenishing the skilled labour force, improving its skills and adapting them to some of the changes in the economy, and it can be an important means of providing more equitable opportunities in education and employment for some young people who would otherwise have been unable to continue their education in school.

Although apprenticeship has proved its value in a number of countries as a system of training and employment its future development in the total context of education, training and employment policies raises complex and difficult problems of policy. The interests and responsibilities of the apprentice and of the qualified craftsman, of the enterprise and of the economy, do not always coincide and may conflict. Employers' decisions about the intake of apprentices are frequently made on the basis of their current needs rather than their longer-term needs or those of the labour force, the industry or the economy. Clearly their decisions cannot easily be adapted to the current increase in the number of young people entering the labour force. Long-term trends in the economy, including those resulting from changing economic relations among countries, developments in technology and organisation, increases in costs or an inability to arrange training without interfering with production, are leading many enterprises to reduce or discontinue long-term skill training. These difficulties have been further compounded by conjunctural changes, especially the recent rise in the level of unemployment, the prospect that it will remain above average for some years and uncertainties about patterns of employment in the future. At the same time the changes taking place or being considered in education, including vocational education in school, and the search for more equitable educational opportunities also call for adaptations in apprenticeship.

MAJOR FEATURES OF APPRENTICESHIP

Apprenticeship is one form of long-term skill training. Its chief distinguishing feature is the existence of a contract between the apprentice, or his legal guardian, and the employer; the apprentice works for the employer at a wage that usually increases during his training, and the employer provides instruction and practice leading to the acquisition of a recognized qualification as a skilled craftsman. The importance of apprenticeship varies widely among countries as a result of historical and institutional factors. This is illustrated by the proportion of apprentices in total employment (Table 1) and also by the proportion of an age-group which enters apprenticeship (Table 2). Differences among countries also appear in the scope of apprenticeship, both among occupations and by occupational level. In some countries apprenticeship is concentrated in relatively few trades or crafts at the level of the skilled worker, while in others it extends among a wide range of varied occupations, from semi-skilled training to technical and sub-professional preparation. A further differentiating factor is the extent to which other training methods, especially vocational education, have affected the proportion of young people who neither proceed with general education nor enter full-time employment directly.

An examination of apprenticeship systems in OECD countries suggests that two main types of apprenticeship have developed. One is found in the English-speaking countries, and the other is the continental European system. The key element in the first model is the importance of craft trade unions in maintaining apprenticeship as part of the private collective bargaining system. Under the influence of the long tradition of apprenticeship in the United Kingdom, the other English-speaking countries have developed similar apprenticeship systems. Ireland, Australia and New Zealand approximate the British model somewhat more closely than Canada and the United States. By contrast, in the continental European countries governments have a more active role, and there is a broader concept of apprenticeable occupations, a greater direction of apprenticeship by employers, fewer limitations on the ratio of apprentices to skilled workers in the enterprise, more emphasis on compulsory related instruction, a larger element of general education, and a more limited role for trade unions. Among the continental European countries apprenticeship remains the chief activity of school-leavers in Germany, Austria and Switzerland. In the other continental European countries, the proportion of school-leavers entering vocational or general education is equal to or greater than the proportion entering apprenticeship. Whilst apprenticeship exists in Scandinavian countries it remains on a relatively small scale, and other forms of vocational training have been developed by public policy, primarily with a view to creating more equitable opportunities in education and employment.

POLICY OBJECTIVES AND OPTIONS

Despite the differences among countries in the role of apprenticeship, many of the policy issues are similar. They can be discussed under seven main considerations:

- the future of apprenticeship;
- the relationship of apprenticeship to education;
- the improvement of apprenticeship training;
- the relationship of apprenticeship to employment;
- the relationship of apprenticeship to other types of training;
- the relationship between the education and manpower authorities; and
- the financing of apprenticeship.

The Future of Apprenticeship

A central question that has to be asked concerns the broad future of apprenticeship. In several countries it is still an important form of vocational preparation. Nevertheless, the reasons for which apprenticeship systems arose are no longer as valid as they used to be, and in several countries this form of vocational training is declining compared with others. It may be important to recognize these trends, and the forces that underlie them, if sufficient thought is to be given to the difficult question of whether and how public policy should support apprenticeship systems or facilitate their replacement by other forms of training.

In some countries the future of apprenticeship is uncertain. Primarily because of their reduced or even negative net benefits or positive costs, many enterprises are unable or unwilling to provide training of any kind, especially long-term initial training. Current and prospective employment conditions, which are more uncertain than usual, have inhibited the creation of new jobs and so have reduced the number of jobs for young people to an unusually low level. Although apprenticeship has many advantages for participants and the economy, few enterprises are able to meet all the training and employment needs of individuals and of the economy at the same time as they satisfy their own; and several governments have experienced difficulty in devising effective policies for dealing with this problem. The ratios between apprentices and skilled workers imposed by trade unions in some countries may be less important in restricting the total intake of apprentices than the fact that many eligible employers offer no apprentice places at all or do not provide places according to the legislated or negotiated levels. Furthermore, questions have been asked about the desirability of enterprises playing a central role in the selection, training and testing of trainees, especially since social disparities can arise when criteria of economic performance alone are used: it is reasonable to assume that governments are better able to take a comprehensive view of the needs of individuals and of the economy, and better able to deploy resources accordingly.

On the other hand it is argued that enterprises are better able than governments to judge detailed employment and training prospects realistically in the light of their engagement in the competitive process, especially in view of the changes taking place in international comparative advantage, and to provide training to a high standard. It is also argued that in many countries vocational education under public auspices has its weaknesses: that vocational education within the education system has not so far been adequately developed and articulated to other forms of education and training; and that since the training policies of the manpower authorities focus primarily on marginal short-term objectives they may not be well equipped to deal with long-term initial training such as apprenticeship.

In countries where a limited range of occupations is apprenticeable, it may be difficult under prospective employment conditions to expand the intake into apprenticeship short of full government financing of net training costs. In Germany there has been considerable success in increasing the number of apprenticeships through an appeal to employers and the threat of a tax. However, the main response in Germany has been from the artisan sector, and it is debatable whether these are the occupations in which training is most needed by individuals and the economy. In France also the major response has been in the craft sector (in 1977, 60 to 65% of apprenticeship contracts were taken up in the craft sector). Although there is general agreement that apprenticeship in any field serves well to introduce young people to working life, for some it may merely postpone the occupational choices and job search which would otherwise occur at the end of schooling.

It is suggested in some countries that apprenticeship should be extended to a larger number of occupations but there is debate about whether it is feasible. In most countries the occupations most suitable for apprenticeship are in the construction trades, repair services for automobiles and similar consumer goods, and in the artisan-type, labour-intensive manufacturing sector. However apprenticeship opportunities in manufacturing have diminished by the decline in the proportion of craftsmen, changes in work organisation and technology and because employment in manufacturing is a declining proportion of total employment in most countries. Among the countries reviewed only the United States has expressed an official interest in enlarging the number and type of apprenticeable occupations to encompass sectors of the economy which have not previously had apprenticeship programmes. While a belief that apprenticeship is a good training method underlies American policy, it is also motivated by the desire to increase the proportion of minority groups, including females, in apprenticeship. The creation of new CAPs (Professional Aptitude Certificates) and the modification of existing ones reflects a similar concern in France. The apprenticeship openings made available in this way are principally in the craft sector. In France, women are strongly represented in certain branches (health and beauty care and sales areas).

More generally, it is clear that vocational education and training has many weaknesses, irrespective of where the locus of responsibility lies. Since much training will continue to occur at the work place, the broader question that arises is how the content and availability of vocational preparation can be improved and the options extended, rather than whether to extend or improve one particular form of it, i.e. apprenticeship. Consideration then has to be given to how these changes might be achieved through new forms of collaborative arrangements to share the respective responsibilities and resources of the education and manpower authorities, employers, workers' representatives and the young people themselves.

The Relationship of Apprenticeship to Education

Almost without exception Member countries agree on the objective that on completing his apprenticeship a qualified craftsman should have the opportunity to resume general education or enter a higher level of vocational education. Some countries also wish to provide a smoother transition from compulsory or upper secondary school to apprenticeship. A growing number of countries seek to incorporate continuing general education into apprenticeship, and to make it compulsory to provide related theoretical instruction. The following main types of action merit consideration toward the achievement of these objectives.

a) Action to make a completed apprenticeship a fully-accredited educational link

Full academic credit can be granted for the general and related theoretical courses taken by apprentices. To this end they can be located within regular academic classes, as in the Kollegstufe of North Rhine-Westphalia in Germany. Conferring simultaneous vocational and educational credentials on the completion of apprenticeship, as is done in Austria, has proved an effective method for forging a link with other forms of education. Another method, used in the United States on an experimental basis, awards academic credit for part of apprenticeship training, enabling apprentices to work towards a two-year degree in a Community College and this, in turn, allows further study for an academic B.A. In France the possibility that those who undertake several different types of vocational preparation can accumulate a series of state-conferred diplomas permits apprentices to proceed to further vocational education and higher vocational diplomas. Thus far, most countries have established better connections with vocational than with academic education, since apprentices have shown more interest in doing so. There appears to be a need and scope for creating easier access to academic education as well.

b) Action to help move from school to apprenticeship

Various linkages have been devised, either within the framework of compulsory education or immediately afterwards, to ease the movement into apprenticeship, draw in young people who might otherwise proceed directly to employment without training, create apprenticeships which might otherwise not exist, improve the occupational information and choices of prospective apprentices, offer a broader initial training than is customary in the first year, and shorten the duration of apprenticeship. Not all of these objectives can be met by a single programme, but some of them are present in recent innovations in a number of countries, depending on their national circumstances, such as pre-apprenticeship in France; the polytechnic final year of compulsory education in Austria; the basic vocational preparation year in Germany; or the EFG programme in Denmark.

c) The provision of continuing general education for apprentices

One of the principles accepted by the Joint Working Party on Education and Working Life* is that all young people should have the opportunity of some form of full-time or part-time education until at least the age of 18. By extension, part of that education should consist

---

* OECD Working Party established in 1975 between the Education Committe, the Manpower and Social Affairs Committee and the Governing Board of the Centre for Educational Research and Innovation.

of general subjects which are useful to young people's development as individuals and as citizens, and to possible further education and training. Countries where part-time education is obligatory for all young people leaving compulsory schooling, or for apprentices, are more apt to provide the general education element than others. Recent developments of interest are the increase in the total amount of time allotted to general and related education within apprenticeship schemes in several countries, the introduction of additional subjects, including sports, and a closer approximation to the patterns and styles of full-time education, including the use of the same school buildings and facilities.

d) Compulsory integrated theoretical education

Almost everywhere it is obligatory for apprentices to be given a certain amount of related instruction away from the enterprise during working hours. This requirement may be imposed by legislation, or through the influence of arrangements among enterprises such as the Industrial Training Boards in the United Kingdom, or through financial inducements, such as government payments to employers or to apprentices for the time spent in school. The willingness of employers to release both apprentices and young workers for part-time general and related instruction seems to be increased when governments assume the costs. The financial burden on the community of full-time education for this group would be greater were it not for the part-time system. A particular problem in several countries has been to integrate the timing and subject matter of instruction in the enterprise, the off-the-job training centre, and the school. In some cases the situation seems to be improved when each type of instruction is arranged on the basis of a "block" release or a "sandwich" course; but this kind of arrangement is not universally favoured for all industries in most countries. In the apprentice training centres in France (CFA - Centres de Formation d'Apprentis), apprentices can receive not only off-the-job practical instruction, but also related education and general subjects. Off-the-job training in other countries may lead to the creation of special centres, although there might be conflict with established part-time government vocational schools. In the United States, where the average age of apprentices is higher than in Europe, related instruction has frequently been outside working hours and entirely at the apprentice's expense.

The Improvement of Apprenticeship Training

Many countries have been modifying the structure and content of apprenticeship training in order to make it correspond better to the longer-term employment needs of the trainees and the economy. In some cases these changes also correspond to the needs of employers, but some employers object to the newer methods. This is because training relates less closely to jobs within their particular enterprises, apprentices spend less time on production, and employers' training costs are considerably increased. It is characteristic of many aspects of apprenticeship that there is no clear-cut harmony of interests among all the participants, not to mention such non-participants as employers who do not give training.

The moves to improve training which are suggested most frequently are as follows.

    a) Apprenticeable occupations may be combined into broader groups or clusters of occupations. This permits a delay in specialization while a broad introduction to related skills is given, perhaps in an introductory year. To this end, the authorities responsible for apprenticeship can consider the suggestion in the report of the Joint Working Party on Education and Working Life that the alternative to occupation as the basis of employment preparation is to adapt training to types of related employment with common or similar work functions.* Such a concept may be an important way of maintaining one of the essential elements of apprenticeship: a degree of versatility which makes the qualified craftsman transferable among enterprises.

    b) Training by stages or modules which can be combined in various ways permits a delay in specialization, and can be a way of reducing time in training and the human costs of failure. However, some trade unions fear that young people may abandon training before they are fully qualified.

    c) Off-the-job training in special centres, sometimes for the entire first year of training, permits a greater degree of standardization of training, compensates for the limited training facilities in small enterprises, and can help meet the difficulty of many enterprises in financing the whole of apprentice training.

    d) "Block release" or "sandwich" courses meet the needs of employers in some industries better than day release for related instruction in schools. In some countries this is also held to be a more effective and economical educational procedure for the apprentices, especially those who live in rural or sparsely settled areas.

    e) The general duration of apprenticeship may be reduced from four years or more to three years or less in order to interest more young people in undertaking apprenticeships and produce more skilled workers for the economy. This can be done without adverse effects on the quality of the training by the

---

* Education and Working Life, OECD, Paris, 1977.

adoption of the other improvements in a) to d) above. Some training experts fear however that apprenticeship may thus become too short. The main obstacle to shorter apprenticeship training is that apprentices would thereby more quickly reach normal pay scales and would be employed less time on productive work. This could discourage some enterprises from providing training, although it might make apprenticeship more attractive to young people, especially if allowance were made for entrants with more basic education and the content of training were related to individual ability and progress.

f) There is also scope in some countries for technical improvements, such as revised syllabuses for training; revised examination and certification systems; better training and preparation of instructors in enterprises and training centres and of the vocational teachers in the schools; improved teaching materials and equipment; and increased and improved teams of outside advisers and inspectors of apprenticeship training. These improvements can be helped by research to find better training methods, experimentation with model training programmes and related activities in research institutes associated with vocational training.

Governments could also seek to influence the social, educational and geographic composition of apprentices. In particular, efforts could be made to broaden the intake from the lower socio-economic groups, lower academic achievers, minority groups, women, the physically and mentally handicapped, and those living in regions where apprenticeships are scarce or undiversified. The action being taken to this end in Germany, France and the United States is worth close attention. It is more difficult to diminish social selectivity by increasing the intake from the higher socio-economic and academic groups because social selectivity is established in an upward direction by selection for academic streams and by the preferences of young people.

The Relationship of Apprenticeship to Employment

In countries where apprenticeship is a major method of training young people, one of its advantages is said to be that employers know their own medium- and longer-term needs for trained manpower much better than those who plan vocational education. There are, however, several limitations in practice to the extent to which employers as a whole provide adequate training, even in pursuit of their own future needs for skilled manpower. These are the high proportion of eligible employers who do little or no training; the need for certain kinds of skilled manpower in industries or enterprises that are unequipped to train at all; the fact that immediate employment requirements may take precedence over training in the intake and training of apprentices; the impact of conjunctural variations on the intake of new apprentices; and the urge to make training specific to the enterprise. All these weaknesses in a system of employer-centred training create a role for public policy. In addition, individual enterprises, even if they are aware of their own training needs, are rarely aware of the future needs of the entire industry or of the economy as a whole or prepared to adjust their training accordingly. Finally, employers in following their own interests are not necessarily meeting the needs, quantitative or qualitative, of young people for whom Member governments have agreed that they have a responsibility to provide vocational preparation. For these reasons, several types of government action, which are being introduced in some countries, are worthy of wider consideration.

a) The total number of apprenticeships can be increased by enlisting employers who currently do not train, and inducing government at all levels and public enterprises to do their share of training.

b) The conjunctural variations in the intake of apprentices can be smoothed out and training and education facilities provided for apprentices who have been laid off. The high level of unemployment to be anticipated in OECD countries calls for the wider application of measures that are being taken to this end.

c) The distribution of apprenticeships among growth industries and occupations, combined with efforts to relate the content of training to common skills can help adapt apprentice training to future needs for skilled manpower. There is a special responsibility on information and counselling services in education and employment to help young people choose training occupations by longer-term criteria than their current popularity.

d) It may to some extent be possible to reduce dropouts during and after apprenticeship by adjusting earnings differentials, especially the narrowing gap between skilled and semi-skilled adults, since in some countries long-run income prospects deter some young people from entering or completing apprenticeship.

e) Employers can be encouraged by the placement service to accept apprentices trained in another, related field. In times of full employment, this substitution may occur spontaneously. Under current employment conditions, more deliberate action is needed.

f) Special incentives might be provided to employers in areas where limited industrial diversity or a low level of economic activity restricts apprenticeship opportunities.

g) Young people in rural areas, or other regions where apprenticeship is limited can be helped take apprenticeships in more developed areas. Appropriate arrangements are required for housing supervision and travel to and from home. An alternative approach is to provide vocational education of a varied character in the home area.

h) There may be a need to modify protective and other legislation (e.g. about working hours) if it seriously reduces employers' willingness to train apprentices. On the other hand young people may be unwilling to train for some occupations unless they have the prospect of better working conditions during their working lives. When considering changes in such legislation countries should examine in detail the potential impact on the availability of apprenticeship opportunities and the willingness of young people to enter them.

i) There is a need to maintain a continuous review and assessment of the content of apprenticeship training so that elements which become obsolete are removed and training better anticipates the conditions that will be in effect when trainees qualify as craftsmen.

j) To provide opportunities for unemployed young people governments could consider purchasing spare training capacity for apprentices in private or public enterprises.

k) Training can be conducted in industry or government centres in periods when employers cannot accept additional apprentices.

l) There is a need to review the number of apprentices who can be hired in relation to the number of skilled workers employed with a view to eliminating unduly restrictive limits.

m) The possibilities can be considered of extending the range of apprenticeable occupations, including a limited form of apprenticeship in occupations which do not require the same length or intensity of skilled training as established arrangements.

n) Financial support can be provided to employers who take on additional apprentices, although it should be noted that cost incentives will only be taken up to the extent that employers expect demand to recover and to create new needs for qualified manpower.

o) There is a need to bring apprenticeship and other methods of skill training into a more coherent relationship within the framework of an overall national policy designed on one hand to give appropriate vocational preparation to all new entrants to the labour force and on the other to provide the skilled manpower needed by the economy.

The Relationship of Apprenticeship to Other Types of Training

In many Member countries apprenticeship is ceasing to be regarded as a separate system, but rather as the first stage of a larger training system which includes other forms of initial training together with a progression of training and retraining opportunities throughout a worker's lifetime. Apprenticeship thus represents only one of the main methods of fulfilling national obligations to offer all young people some form of initial vocational preparation. However, because capacity is limited to expand apprenticeship to meet all the initial training needs of young people and of the economy, and because alternative training methods may be better for some occupations and some young people, countries need to examine how apprenticeship can better be linked to the other ways of preparing young people for entry into working life in the context of the development of an overall strategy for training. These other elements include:

a) Vocational education in public educational institutions. This may be a full-time alternative, but off-the-job training also has an increasing role during the first year of apprenticeship.
b) Formal training by employers other than by apprenticeship which may or may not lead to a recognized qualification.
c) Vocational education in institutions combined with periods of practical experience in an enterprise.
d) Government training programmes.
e) Proprietary vocational schools (in some countries).
f) Armed Forces training.
g) Home study or correspondence courses.

In establishing an overall allocation among the alternative types of initial training, one problem is that they compete for places in enterprises where practical experience can be obtained. Since the importance of a practical component is increasingly recognized in school-based vocational education, it should be anticipated that many employers may prefer candidates for short periods of experience rather than apprentices whose training takes several years.

Study combined with work, in the education system and organised on an alternating or sandwich principle, is worthy of consideration as an alternative to school-bound vocational education, especially in the commercial and services sectors. Co-operative education in the United States and programmes in several other countries at somewhat higher occupational levels illustrate the directions this form of vocational preparation can take.

Member countries, apart from the United States and Canada, tend to concentrate apprenticeship on school-leavers, whether or not the country has legislative or administrative age limits in regard to entering or completing apprenticeship. This arrangement causes relatively few difficulties in those countries, chiefly the continental European ones, that provide alternative opportunities for those who missed apprenticeship in youth or need retraining as skilled workers, provided there are no restrictions on who may be hired as a skilled worker and no requirements that a completed apprenticeship should precede skilled status. Some of the English-speaking countries are concerned about the limited age groups in apprenticeship because craft union restrictions on the acquisition of skilled status require a completed apprenticeship. Such countries seek to extend the age of entrance to apprenticeship and to have alternative training methods accepted.

The Relationship between the Education and Manpower Authorities

Although many people are currently arguing that education and training should be seen as a continuum, in the real world governments and enterprises have their own interests and policies. The dichotomy between the worlds of education and employment is nowhere more apparent than in apprenticeship, whose very essence is to straddle the two. The Report of the Joint Working Party on Education and Working Life warns that "an awareness of the extent to which education and working life operate within different systems becomes therefore crucially important, and particularly when considering coordination not only among government departments, but also between and among the various levels of government and those of enterprises and workers' representatives". *

The choices made by countries about the locus of the primary regulation of apprenticeship vary according to the size and scope of the apprenticeship programme, its traditions, and current aims in regard to apprenticeship. Some countries choose the national education authority as the leading policy body. Others give precedence to a Ministry of Labour, Industry or Economics, or divide the functions among ministries of economics, labour and education. Still others create quasi-public bodies on which employers and trade unions are heavily represented. Most apprenticeship programmes recognize the importance of working arrangements at the regional or local level for the actual conduct of daily affairs; and they too can be governmental, quasi-public or informal.

Whatever choice is made about primary responsibility there is a need at all levels of government for better coordination between the education and manpower authorities in the implementation of apprenticeship policies and their relation with alternative methods of training young people. Again the view of the Joint Working Party is relevant:

* Education and Working Life, OECD, Paris, 1977.

"... collaboration is a process that entails the discussion and reconciliation of different interests and that is not necessarily assured by creating institutions". * The Joint Working Party recommends that the highest levels of government should call upon all ministries and levels of government to take their objectives for education and working life into full consideration in the application and management of all their policies, services and programmes. Such action in relation to apprenticeship would be valuable.

Financing Apprenticeship

The traditional arrangements by which individual or groups of employers have borne the costs of training apprentices have proved unsatisfactory because many eligible employers do no training and benefit from training done by others. Moreover, the increasing costs of apprenticeship, due in part to rising training standards imposed by government, have raised questions about the need for public financial support if apprenticeship is to survive or grow. Various forms of collective financing have been tried in order to provide more and better apprenticeship training.

a) Employers who do not train or train enough are taxed and the receipts are used either to support employers who train or a common training centre for a group of enterprises.
b) All employers are taxed and the proceeds are redistributed either in proportion to the training effort or to encourage additional training.
c) Taxes are levied under specific circumstances when the number of training places appears to be inadequate.

Member countries which have some form of collective financing as well as others have felt pressures to introduce government financial support for apprenticeship. Public financial incentives to maintain or increase the number of apprenticeship places during conjunctural downturns are most common. Over the longer run, as the structure of apprenticeship training has changed, leaving less time for production in the enterprise, and as the excess of benefits over costs has become smaller and even negative, the rationale for a contribution from society has grown. It has been supported further by efforts to incorporate apprenticeship into the educational system and by the recognition that were it not for apprenticeship society would have a larger expenditure on full-time education.

Countries that are concerned about provision for young people may wish to consider programmes to improve or expand apprenticeship

---

* Education and Working Life, OECD, Paris, 1977.

simultaneously with other methods of preparing young people for working life. Special administrative arrangements may be required in countries where separate departments or ministries have jurisdiction, according to whether a programme is education or employer-based. In view of the fact that education-based programmes of occupational skill training are growing faster than apprenticeship or other employer-based programmes in virtually every country, there is an urgent need to examine all the alternative approaches within the context of an overall training policy which reconciles educational and employment considerations and the interests of trainees, employers and the economy.

I

INTRODUCTION

Most OECD countries have long had an apprenticeship system which, to a greater or lesser degree, has provided initial training and occupational skills for young people. The report of the Secretary-General's Group of Experts entitled "Education and Working Life in Modern Society" states that apprenticeship "has substantial virtue in that it gives operational reality to the concept of closer relationships between education and working life, and, at its best, can ensure that work experience brings both personal fulfilment and development... we believe that there is a role for a modern form of apprenticeship...". However, the Report also specifies several defects in apprenticeship and declares that "the traditional schemes are urgently in need of review". (1)*

This report analyses some of the main features, trends and policy issues in apprenticeship in OECD countries. It is timely to assess the position of apprenticeship because, in recent years, many OECD countries have revised their apprenticeship systems through major legislation and improved administration and regulation. Current interest in apprenticeship is high on several grounds, in addition to the traditional one of looking to apprenticeship to provide initial training in a specified range of occupations. Among the factors which have increased and broadened the interest in apprenticeship are perceived difficulties in the transition from school to work in countries where apprenticeship does not encompass a high proportion of early school leavers; young people's dissatisfaction with the final years of compulsory school; a turning away from manual work and some of the crafts; a belief that prolonged education is producing more entrants to the labour force than can be absorbed in the jobs considered suitable to their level of education; in some countries, a bulge in the age group, placing pressure on all education-training facilities over the next years; and, more immediately, the effects of the recession on the intake of apprentices, producing fears of insufficient skill training for the future needs of the economy.

In light of these concerns, apprenticeship systems are called upon to fulfil multiple purposes both for individuals and the society. These purposes are to:

* See References, page 83.

a) replenish or enlarge the skilled labour supply;
b) provide initial training for young people;
c) ease the transition from school to work;
d) introduce young people to working life;
e) promote skill training and access to skilled jobs for groups which are disadvantaged in employment: i.e. low academic achievers, the physically, mentally and socially handicapped, minorities, and females;
f) offer part-time continuing education, at relatively low cost to the government, for those who might otherwise terminate their studies completely;
g) provide equivalent qualifications and alternative routes into upper secondary and tertiary education;
h) regulate the supply and pay of skilled labour.

Not all of the purposes are recognized in every OECD country and some of them are more important than others. In most countries the first two purposes are dominant. However, an appraisal of trends, developments and problems must recognize all of these sometimes competing motives in the policy of governments. The full range of purposes will therefore be considered since this report analyses current apprenticeship practices and suggests possible future lines of development.

OECD countries vary considerably in the scope and importance they attribute at present to apprenticeship as a skill training method. Data about the total number of apprentices as a proportion of total civilian employment in OECD countries indicate that Austria, Germany and Switzerland are the strongholds of apprenticeship; while in Spain, Finland and the United States the incidence of apprenticeship is low, and Sweden has only the vestigial remains of apprenticeship (Table 1). These differences among countries reflect differences in many factors. For example the scope of apprenticeable occupations, the proportion of employers eligible to offer apprenticeship and the proportion of eligible employers actually offering apprenticeship vary considerably. The ratio of apprentices to skilled workers or to training instructors, the duration of apprenticeship, the size of the age group eligible for apprenticeship as a proportion of total employment and employment in the apprenticeable occupations as a share of total employment are other factors which differ. The extent of unregistered apprenticeship (a factor in only a few countries), the utilization of alternative occupational skill training methods, changes in compulsory education laws, voluntary continuation of education beyond compulsory schooling, and the proportion of young people who enter work directly from compulsory education are also important factors underlying the differences among countries.

Table 1. THE INCIDENCE OF APPRENTICESHIP IN SELECTED OECD COUNTRIES, 1974

COUNTRY	NUMBER OF APPRENTICES 000's	APPRENTICES AS A % OF TOTAL CIVILIAN EMPLOYMENT
Australia	131	2.3
Austria	164	5.4
Belgium	18	0.5
Canada	67[a]	0.7
Denmark	32	1.4
Finland	3	0.2
France	197	0.9
Germany	1,130	5.2
Ireland	15	1.4
Italy	670	3.6
Netherlands	70	1.5
New Zealand	32	2.7
Norway[b]	10	0.7
Spain	8	0.1
Sweden	1	c
Switzerland	143	4.9
United Kingdom	463[d]	2.1
United States	291	0.3

NOTES: a) Excluding apprenticeship in Quebec.
 b) 1970.
 c) Under 0.1%.
 d) Great Britain: 1971 Census, Economic Activity, Part II, Tables 2, 10. Number of apprentices in Great Britain estimated from category "Apprentices, articled clerks and formal trainees".

SOURCES: National data and OECD.

Apprenticeship can also be analysed as one of several alternatives open to an age-group. They are extended general education, including tertiary levels; occupational skill training through the educational system or other methods, and direct entrance into employment with little or no formal training provided by employers (Table 2). If OECD countries are classified according to the importance of apprenticeship as an outlet for young people leaving compulsory schooling, four groups may be distinguished:

   i) countries where apprenticeship is the single most important activity of young people after the end of compulsory schooling (Austria, Germany, Switzerland);
  ii) countries where direct entrance to employment is more important than apprenticeship, but where these alternatives together account for a majority of young people of school-leaving age (e.g. Australia, Ireland and the United Kingdom);
 iii) countries where apprenticeship exists, but is secondary to other methods of providing occupational skills to young people (e.g. France and the United States); and
  iv) countries where apprenticeship is almost non-existent or has been confined to training for the ownership or management of small businesses, or is under-developed (e.g. Belgium, Japan, Spain and Sweden).

This report analyses apprenticeship in groups i) to iii) only.

This report does not describe apprenticeship in full nor recapitulate country profiles (2). On particular issues, examples will be cited to illustrate the varied approaches of OECD countries, but no attempt is made to present the situation in each OECD country on each issue. Consideration is given not only to the formal provisions, but also to the actual operation of apprenticeship systems. The main features of apprenticeship and the differences among countries will be examined with regard to:

   a) the legal framework and administrative structure;
   b) the number and type of apprenticeable occupations;
   c) admission to apprenticeship;
   e) examination and certification; and
   f) financing of training.

Part II of this paper deals with the main features of apprenticeship. In Part III the most important recent developments, current issues and problems in apprenticeship are set forth. Statistical information on trends and features of apprenticeship are contained in the Appendix.

Table 2. ACTIVITIES OF YOUNG PEOPLE ON LEAVING COMPULSORY SCHOOL IN SELECTED OECD COUNTRIES, PROPORTION OF SCHOOL LEAVERS IN EACH ACTIVITY

Percentages

COUNTRY	YEAR	FULL-TIME GENERAL EDUCATION	VOCATIONAL EDUCATION	APPRENTICESHIP	WORK OR UNEMPLOYMENT	OTHERS AND UNKNOWN	TOTAL
	1	2	3	4	5	6	7
Austria[b]	1976	14.8	24.3	53.5	7.4		100
Germany[a]	1976	47.8		46.2	2.7	3.3	100
Switzerland[b]	1975	17.0		55.0	28.0		100
Australia[b]	1975	24.0		15.0	61.0		100
England and Wales[b]	1974	20.8		17.8	51.1	10.4	100
Finland[b]	1975	..	77.7	2.1	..		100
France[b]	1975	33.3	31.2	12.5	23.0		100
Ireland[c]	1975	26.0		10.0	59.0	5.0	100
Denmark[c]	1973	65.0	3.0	15.0	15.0	2.0	100
Netherlands[b]	1968/69	75.0		3.0	18.0	4.0	100
United States[d]	1972	51.5	8.0	2.4	28.0[e]	10.1	100

NOTES:
a) Plans of school leavers aged 15-19 (mostly 15-16). Includes Gymnasia leavers of which there were 133,314 out of a total of 888,949 leavers.
b) Age 15-16 or completion of compulsory school.
c) Age 16, completion of school beyond compulsory.
d) Plans of seniors in high school, mostly 17-18 years old.
e) Includes other vocational training.

SOURCES: National data.

II

MAIN FEATURES OF APPRENTICESHIP

A. Legal Framework and Administrative Structure

Official definitions of apprenticeship vary, but on the whole they refer to formal arrangements for initial skill training of a systematic long-term character in a recognized occupation. The training must be both transferable and all-round. The training is centred in an enterprise but has a component of instruction in an institution. It involves a contract of indenture between, on the one hand, the trainee and his or her legal representative and, on the other, a private or public employer, a joint training committee of management or labour, a trade union, a public or quasi-public training organisation, or some other recognized training body. Either by statute or collective agreements, a precise list of apprenticeable occupations has been established, and it excludes formal training which occurs outside these occupations or is conducted in a manner which does not conform to the apprenticeship regulations.

In rare instances, apprenticeship may take place entirely in recognized institutions with facilities for practical work, as in Switzerland. Apprenticeship, in its legal and practical aspects, should be distinguished from other forms of work-study offered either by employers or by the education system.

1. Legislative Provisions

Apprenticeship is generally voluntary in OECD countries and neither employers nor young people are obliged to participate. However, in some countries there are compulsory elements. In some Australian States young people entering certain occupations can be trained only through apprenticeship. In West Germany young people under 18 may only be trained in apprenticeable occupations. In several Canadian Provinces licences or certificates of qualification must be obtained by those who wish to practise enumerated trades; and their laws usually make apprenticeship the principal method of preparing for licensing, although exceptions are made for those who have obtained satisfactory qualifications in other ways or abroad.

In most countries where apprenticeship exists national statutes govern or relate to almost all aspects of it. The United Kingdom is exceptional in having no legislation on apprenticeship directly, although the Industrial Training Act of 1964 and its amendments in 1973 directly affects certain aspects of apprenticeship. In some federal countries state legislation on apprenticeship supplements federal statutes, but in others the states are the predominant or sole source of legal authority. In Canada the federal government leaves almost all aspects to the Provinces, except for financial assistance and a committee that sponsors interprovincial certification of skilled status in selected occupations in order to reconcile the different Provincial systems of training and certification.

In some countries employers offer apprenticeship training or something closely akin to it but do not register the contracts. These unregistered apprenticeships are not illegal and are notable in the United States and parts of Canada. They arise because the benefits of registration seem to be outweighed by the requirements and costs of conforming to all the official regulations. Most unregistered apprenticeships depart in some significant respect from the official rules, but it is not clear that training is inferior for this reason. In the United States it is estimated that perhaps one-third to one-half as many unregistered apprentices as registered ones exist. This contribution to skill training should not be ignored and any programme to expand apprenticeship should consider means of expanding unregistered apprenticeship training whether or not it is brought into the formal system.

Apprenticeship legislation and implementing regulations or decrees usually cover the following subjects: the qualifications, rights, and duties of employers, training officers and apprentices; the content, notification and registration of apprenticeship indentures, contracts or agreements; criteria or procedures for defining apprenticeable trades; the structure of administrative and advisory organisations which plan, conduct, supervise and inspect apprenticeship; the formulation of trade training plans and the organisation and curricula of related education; the duration and completion of apprenticeship and provisions for legal terminations; hours of work, holidays, occupational safety, and other working conditions of apprentices; the amount of pay or how remuneration is to be determined; and examination and certification. Some of these matters may be covered in other legislation, such as protective or safety laws, which may carry specific provisions for apprentices or young workers.

2. Administrative Structures

In OECD countries where comprehensive apprenticeship legislation prevails and related general and theoretical education are obligatory (the "dual" system), a characteristic administrative structure is found. One or more government departments or ministries at the national level may have overall responsibility and also perform specific tasks, aided by specialist bodies and advisory councils on which employer and trade union representatives are prominent. In federal countries, the states may have complete authority over certain aspects or much of the responsibility for carrying out federal regulations may be delegated to them.

A vital part of the administrative apparatus in West Germany, Austria, Denmark and France is the system of Chambers of employers in which membership may be compulsory. These bodies may be divided into industry, commerce, and artisan trades or may be unified, as in Austria. The Chambers have regional and local divisions which in effect operate apprenticeship on a day-to-day basis, under government supervision. Austria is unusual in that there is also a legally established Chamber of Labour at federal level that influences overall policy and specific issues. However, at the operating level, the apprenticeship centres (Lehrlingsstellen) are established under the sole authority of the employers' Chamber, and trade unions have urged a new organisation in which they would have equal representation. In France public enterprises, occupational associations and other bodies also have some regulatory authority. In the Netherlands, each branch of industry has a central training organisation which regulates apprenticeship through a Foundation consisting of employer and union representatives from all the denominational groups active in Dutch life.

In Switzerland, the cantonal authorities are in charge of organising and administering apprenticeship and they use public or semi-public bodies on which employers and trade unions are officials or advisers. Similar provisions exist in the Canadian provinces and the Australian states and territories. Ireland revoked the 1959 Apprenticeship Act in 1967 and established an industrial training authority, AnCO, with overall responsibility for apprenticeship and other manpower training. The Council of AnCO has representatives of employers, trade unions and educational interests as well as government departments. In Finland, the Ministry of Education and the National Board of Education have the main responsibility and there are 28 apprenticeship councils for different occupations in which government, labour and vocational education authorities sit. Local supervision and control is vested in the municipal authorities. In the United States there are about 7,000 joint apprenticeship and training committees which constitute a major force in initiating and conducting apprenticeship. They are composed equally of management and labour representatives, and account for the training of 68% of the registered apprentices, although they represent only 17% of the total registered programmes (10).

B. Number and Type of Apprenticeable Occupations

The type and number of occupations considered suitable for apprenticeship training vary considerably among the OECD countries. Countries also differ in their actual utilization of apprenticeship in the apprenticeable occupations and in their degree and rate of substitution of alternative forms of training. Within each country the number of apprenticeable occupations changes at intervals as obsolete occupations are removed, new ones are added, and occupations are redefined and combined. In practice they are more frequently combined than differentiated and split. The German list has been shortened from 600 in 1969 to 465. The Austrian list was reduced from 300 in 1970 to 225 in July 1975. Denmark has 160 occupations on its list and France has 270 occupations in which the CAP examinations may be taken. The United States, contrary to the general trend, has increased its total number of apprenticeable occupations in recent years.

In the continental European countries the legislative and actual coverage of their apprenticeship systems extend to all kinds of jobs in offices, sales, banks, insurance companies, travel and tourist offices, hotels and restaurants, laboratories, medical and dental offices as well as the more usual craft and artisan occupations recognized in all countries with apprenticeship systems. Some countries include the training of technicians and sub-professionals and some embrace semi-skilled trades, offering shorter training and a lesser status. The Austrian trade unions are urging that the reform of vocational training legislation now being debated should extend apprenticeship to skills which can be acquired in less than two years on the grounds that present conditions discriminate against certain groups of young people. Employers oppose the suggested change, arguing that present on-the-job training for semi-skilled workers functions well.

In Ireland, Australia and the United Kingdom there is a more restricted conception of the occupations which are suitable for apprenticeship. In Ireland AnCO has designated as apprenticeable only 7 major trades comprising under 50 occupations and has stated explicitly that "... AnCO inherited the present apprenticeship system. Had this system not existed, it is unlikely that training schemes based on apprenticeship would now be proposed to cater for the training of skilled workers. Similarly, the Australian response to the OECD questionnaire on apprenticeship declares that "if industry were to be restructured it is likely that the traditional apprenticeship system would not be adopted and that much more flexible arrangements would result". Under Australian conditions it has been argued that the "trowel" trades of the building industry, because of the skills involved and the amount of sub-contracting and piece-work in the industry, would provide better training outside apprenticeship. The formal and regulated nature of apprenticeship has also been called unsuitable to welding, hairdressing, locksmithing, food services and a number of minor trades.

In France, the existence of full-time vocational education as a competing method of preparing for most of the apprenticeable occupations has made apprenticeship a residual method of skill training which is chosen by the least academic young people and stresses the least technical occupations. Even in the countries where apprenticeship is still an important training method in many occupations, the competing methods of occupational preparation have grown at a more rapid rate than apprenticeship in recent years. Particularly in the occupations entered by girls, full-time vocational education has become an alternative and often preferred method of preparation. It is also prominent in the occupations where the content is more theoretical than practical and in new occupations, especially in the services. In several countries the shift would be even more marked if the number of places in educational institutions had expanded in response to the demand. Several thousand young Austrians have settled for apprenticeships in recent years, although their first choice was to attend vocational schools (Appendix, Table 3). Apprenticeship is of minor importance as a training method in the United States compared with on-the-job experience, special training within the firm, and occupational courses in high schools, community colleges, and proprietary institutions. Even in the narrow area of craft-workers, registered apprenticeships provide only 45,000 new journeymen a year for jobs where estimates say 400,000 new skilled employees are needed each year (10).

No matter how broad and long the list of apprenticeable occupations is, each country tends to develop concentration patterns: a high proportion of apprentices clusters in a few occupations, according to the training opportunities available, current fashions in popular trades, and the attractiveness of the pay and other working conditions. The preferences of young people and the geographical distribution of apprenticeship openings are such that even in times when the total number of openings is smaller than the number seeking apprenticeships, some openings tend to remain unfilled. Research in Germany has indicated that the apprenticeship vacancies offered by employers do not conform to the skill requirements of the economy (24). Moreover, young people's choices of an apprenticeship occupation are determined primarily by what is available to them locally, since they are generally too young to move. An improvement of the selection of places and a reduction in the competition for the most desirable apprenticeships would do more for better choices than improved occupational information services. Youthful preferences as expressed in surveys are, however, not closely related to the skills that are in demand in employment, but seem to follow a popularity curve. Occupational information might improve this situation. Changes of apprenticeship occupation and dropouts during training are due to some extent to poor knowledge of the occupation, but an equal cause is that some apprentices are obliged to enter an occupation or firm that was not their first choice.

C. Admission to Apprenticeship

1. Age of Entry and Completion

Legislative provisions range from those which specify that apprenticeship must be entered and completed during certain years to those which make no mention of age at all. A minimum age for entry is often specified, usually coinciding with the end of compulsory education. Most OECD countries have no legal limitations on the upper entry age to apprenticeship and do not specify when apprenticeship must be completed. Nevertheless, in most of them apprenticeship begins at 15-16, and ends in the teenage years. Few young people over 20 enter apprenticeship except in Canada and the United States.

In some countries where the age of entry and completion are regulated by collective agreements (usually involving craft union) on the conditions of apprenticeship, rather than by legal provisions, school-leavers are favoured, and those 21 and over may be excluded in some occupations (United Kingdom, Ireland, Australia). In the United Kingdom, the major effort is directed toward gaining union acceptance for adults trained in government skill centres. In most countries adult workers who were trained through apprenticeship and desire or need to bring their skills up-to-date are given such courses outside apprenticeship.

In Ireland, an effort to expand apprenticeship to adults has involved exemptions from age restrictions in specific collective agreements, started official discussions on the age limits, and instituted three adult apprenticeship schemes in local areas. The Council of AnCO also decided in 1975 that "in areas where there is rapid industrial growth and a shortage of craftsmen, AnCO, in co-operation with the National Manpower Service, shall take positive action and initiate discussions with trade union and employer interests aimed at establishing craft courses for adults in approved training centres in these areas" (4). Although an upper age limit for entry to apprenticeship exists in only one Australian state, in practice most apprenticeships must be completed before the trainee becomes 23 years of age. The Australian authorities report that the parties to federal awards have made no move to liberalize conditions and have jealously retained the power of determining these aspects of apprenticeship. Although age restrictions have been set aside on occasion when labour market shortages appeared to warrant training of older entrants as apprentices, the major thrust in adult training and retraining has occurred outside the apprenticeship system. One of the chief obstacles to including adults in apprenticeship has been union insistence on adult wage levels. Federal training allowances have been used as a supplement in some cases.

Most OECD countries see no objection to the concentration of apprenticeship on young people. Those in which apprenticeship constitutes the training method for an overwhelming proportion of skilled workers (e.g. Austria, Germany, Switzerland) feel no need for positive measures to open apprenticeship to adults as long as adult skill training exists and is accepted. In Austria, adults over 21 who have acquired skills through work experience and education may take the final apprenticeship examination without going through apprenticeship. In countries where alternative methods of acquiring skills in youth and adulthood have wide acceptance (e.g. Denmark, France, Finland, the Netherlands and Norway) little need is seen to change the present age concentration of apprenticeship.

2. Standards of Entry

The completion of compulsory education is usually specified as a minimum requirement for admission to apprenticeship. Some countries stipulate certain levels of academic achievement in designated subjects, or have aptitude and other tests, and other selection procedures. In Ireland, AnCO must approve each applicant for apprenticeship. The Employment Service often aids employers by conducting such tests even where no legal provision exists. Many employers use their own screening measures. Employers' standards for admission rise when the supply of young people increases faster than the openings (5). Minimum admission standards tend to be lower in the countries which have a broad list of apprenticeable occupations than in those where skilled crafts training for industry predominates. In every country visited, some employers considered that entering apprentices were inadequately prepared at school in the basic skills of computation, comprehension, and communication. Remedial classes are offered in the workshop, in a group training centre, or in the educational institution that provides the theoretical part of the programme. Employers consider that basic preparation is the task of the school, and object to having to provide this kind of training.

In some countries, and for some kinds of apprenticeships, the length of the apprenticeship may be reduced for the older entrant who has had a longer general education or an introductory vocational education. Although practice is varied, the tendency is to give more credit for vocational education than for general education. Previous work experience may qualify an apprentice for a reduction of time; but, in fact, relatively few apprentices have worked before starting their training except in Canada and the United States.

Many studies have established that apprentices are drawn disproportionately from the lower socio-economic classes, but less so than those young people who enter employment direct from compulsory school or soon thereafter. Danish data for 1973 are particularly clear on this point (6). Nor is apprenticeship itself an entirely uniform category. Analyses of the academic and social background of apprentices show a high correlation with the type of apprenticeship entered, rated by prestige, career prospects, and the difficulty of the theoretical component (7). Certain types of prestigious apprenticeships in Germany and Austria are entered predominantly by young people who have gone further than compulsory general education.

3. Limits to Recruitment

It is an essential part of all apprenticeship training regulations that an adequate number of qualified instructors should be in charge of the training and that no firm should hire more apprentices than it can train. In some countries artisan firms can be established only by qualified master craftsmen. Two groups of countries may be distinguished: those which usually regulate an employer's intake and total number of apprentices by the number of skilled men he employs in production (taken separately for each apprenticeable occupation); and those which stipulate that the firm must employ a certain number of persons qualified to train particular types of apprentices. In the latter case, full-time and part-time instructors who have no production functions at all may form the basis of the apprenticeship ratio. Legislated, negotiated and actual ratios vary (Appendix, Tables 5-8). In many countries the legally prescribed ratios between the number of apprentices and the number of skilled workers or persons qualified to train apprentices in the enterprise vary according to occupation. In federal countries variations are also found within the same occupation among provinces or states. Negotiated ratios, set by collective bargaining agreements (or industrial awards and determinations in Australia), frequently differ from the legal ratios and take precedence. Negotiated ratios reflect the current employment situation, projected employment prospects for skilled workers and other conditions of concern to trade unions, and are more prevalent in the English-speaking countries than in the continental European countries. Actual ratios in an occupation are usually lower than negotiated or legal ratios because they take account of eligible employers who do not train at all or train below the legal or negotiated level, and are also affected by such factors as the unavailability of suitable apprentices or local trade union procedures that limit intake.

The training regulations established by government in Austria and West Germany are couched in terms of the maximum permissible number of apprentices in relation to the number of persons qualified to give instruction, and no apprenticeship contract which does not take these ratios into account may be registered. However, under this system ratios can be changed easily to conform to new circumstances, since an employer can expand his apprenticeship intake by hiring more training instructors, especially if the firm maintains an apprentice training centre or corner apart from the production process. Trade unions in these countries, because of their industrial structure and the long-standing shortages of skilled workers, do not object to an expansion of apprentice intake by individual employers. In fact, few questions are raised about the ability of all apprentices to continue as skilled workers in the particular occupations for which they have trained. Apprenticeship is viewed as a valuable introduction to working life, there is no great concern if apprentices are employed in occupations other than their specialization, and a general attitude that "you cannot have too many skilled workers" prevails.

Most of the English-speaking countries set ratios by collective agreements between employers and trade unions. The latter are generally resistant to changes in the ratios, citing concern for the adequacy of training as the chief reason for limiting the intake of apprentices. However, this argument does not take account of the unavailability or inability of some skilled workers in an enterprise to give training, nor of new methods and places of training which are independent of skilled persons in the production process. An additional reason for limiting the number of apprentices is the desire of craft unions to safeguard the employment of members who complete apprenticeship and to avoid training new apprentices when skilled workers are unemployed. Many employers are not training at all or are not up to the ratios prescribed, so that union limitations are not the primary restraint. A few employers may be able and willing to train more apprentices than unions permit, but this is unusual. When a government or an industry training authority foresees an impending shortage of skilled workers and wishes to expand apprenticeship and the unions, governed by immediate and local considerations, refuse to change the apprenticeship ratios, problems arise. Discussions and negotiations on these ratios constitute an important part of AnCO's effort to expand Irish apprenticeship. In Australia, the long-standing arrangements on ratios have most commonly prescribed not more than one apprentice to three tradesmen but, with the agreement of the apprenticeship authority, this provision can be varied, and Australian officials state that employers who have adequate or more than adequate training facilities rarely fail to obtain agreement to train more apprentices than the standard ratio.

Differences in the ratios established from one country to another for identical occupations suggest that a new examination of the subject and a sharing of experience among countries might be beneficial. Even within a country, the ratios vary from occupation to occupation, and the differences are not entirely explicable in training terms.

4. Termination before Completion

Many countries provide for a probationary period during which either party may terminate the apprenticeship without penalty. Post-probationary terminations without justifiable cause constitute a breach of contract, but the degree of enforcement and the range of acceptable reasons for termination vary widely among countries. Failure to attend prescribed training or school sessions may automatically result in termination in several countries. In addition, there is a great variation in the amount of effort devoted to placing with other employers the apprentices of employers who have failed in business or who are unable to maintain training for economic reasons.

Statistics on cancelled apprenticeships seem to be collected and published more frequently by the English-speaking countries than by others. In the United States cancellations during 1975 constituted just over 20% of the total number of apprentices in training at the end of the year. Canadian cancellations in 1974-75, excluding Quebec, were 13.3% of the number of apprentices at the end of the training year. In New Zealand, the cancellation rate ranged from 7 to 11% during the years 1969-1976. In Australia where the cancellation rate for 1975-76 was only 5.2% reasons for cancellations indicate that "loss of interest", defined as leaving for another occupation or an unsatisfactory work record, accounted for 38% of the cancellations. As the second most important cause, a miscellaneous "other" is given, including financial pressures to earn more and marriage (for females). Misconduct (absconding, conviction in court of law, neglect of technical course), incapacity (death, illness, injury), change of residence and training problems (including economic inability of employer to provide work) follow in that order and each account for under 10% of the total (8). In many countries cancellations are more frequently initiated by apprentices than by employers. Although apprentices as well as employers are bound by contracts, an employer rarely tries to get legal satisfaction when an apprentice leaves voluntarily.

In Denmark the dropout rate is heaviest during the first six months when the probation period enables either side to cancel without reason or notice. Authorities believe that the chief cause of dropping-out is an uninformed choice of a training occupation. An experimental programme (EFG) to provide introductory information and knowledge was started in the 1960s and extended under the vocational training act of 1972. It is planned that a year of basic vocational education should follow the end of primary school and should count as the first year of apprenticeship. Other countries have also introduced new educational information and guidance programmes to improve the occupational choices and completion rates of apprentices.

It is another matter to establish what proportion of those who begin an apprenticeship programme will complete it and earn whatever credentials are awarded. Only 1% of all Irish apprentices are said to fail to complete their full term which is long by international standards. A high wastage rate occurs during the training period in the British engineering industries, a broad group of industries encompassing over 3 million workers (9). In the United States it is estimated that half the entrants fail to complete their apprenticeship. In Canada and the United States an important cause of apprenticeship not being completed is the irregularity of employment in the construction industry. There are frequent periods of lay-off for apprentices when work is slack. Conversely American apprentices are able to obtain satisfactory pay and skilled status in boom times without completing an apprenticeship.

5. Admission of Special Groups

Many special efforts are being made to recruit to apprenticeship females, minorities, the handicapped, the less academically able, deprived working class, young people, and those living in areas of restricted economic opportunity. Several countries are concerned about the opportunities for each of these groups and the programmes to expand their participation in apprenticeship.

Three main points can be made about girls and apprenticeship.

a) Females are underrepresented in apprenticeship in relation to their share of the labour force. The degree of underrepresentation tends to be lower in countries where a broad list of apprenticeable occupations exists and female-intensive occupations are included.

b) No market trend in the female share is visible, either within or among countries.

c) Female apprentices are concentrated in fewer training occupations than males and often in female-intensive, less skilled occupations. This feature is particularly conspicuous in countries which have a long list of apprenticeable occupations.

The barriers to further participation by females are rarely legal or administrative. A large residue of resistance among the trainers remains. Just as significant is the continued disinterest on the part of girls and their parents in apprenticeship and in training in male-intensive occupations. As the length of training is shortened, girls may be more attracted to apprenticeship. Recent official initiatives to open more apprenticeship places and occupations to females mark a new period, that cannot be judged for some time.

Race and ethnicity as obstacles to admission to apprenticeship have been far more prominent as a public issue in the United States than in other countries, but attention has also been given in the United Kingdom and in some continental countries, especially Germany, in relation to the children of foreign workers. The minority groups designated in the United States - Blacks, Orientals, American Indians, Spanish-speaking - have increased from 6% of all apprentices in 1968 to 18.1% in 1976, and the percentage rose even in years when the total number of apprentices declined. At the end of 1975, minority apprentices in each of 19 occupations constituted 20% or more of the total, with the highest proportions of minority apprentices in the following: cement mason, cook or baker, plasterer, roofer, and operating engineer (10, 41). The increases are attributable to the enforcement of equal employment opportunity requirements by federal and state apprenticeship authorities and the apprenticeship outreach programmes which were pioneered by the Workers Defense League, beginning in 1964 (12, 41).

As a programme essentially catering for young people, apprenticeship has not had to cope with many foreign workers themselves; but the children of some foreign workers or immigrants who have had an incomplete education in the host country or have finished school later than the normal age pose problems. The British experience during the 1960s with West Indian, African, Pakistani and Indian youngsters indicated that when economic conditions were favourable, colour discrimination could be overcome by determined placement efforts of the Careers Service, and age limits could be set aside for coloured young people who were equal in ability to British apprentices. However, as the unemployment of young people has risen in recent years, the situation for coloured school-leavers has deteriorated. A variety of approaches by official agencies has been used to ensure a fair share of apprenticeships for them. In Germany the high birth rate in families of foreign workers increased the number of such pupils attending German schools from 35,100 in 1965-66 to half a million in 1975-76. Currently about three-fifths of these children leave compulsory school without a diploma, and usually have language problems which exclude them from normal apprenticeships. The Federal Ministry of Labour has devised special one-year courses to prepare young people of foreign birth or parentage to enter apprenticeship, supplementing special educational efforts of the Federal Ministry of Education. Some states also have special language and remedial programmes (13).

The possibility that apprenticeship might offer opportunities to physically and mentally handicapped young people has been raised in several countries. In Germany, Krupp and other large employers pioneered the setting up of shorter apprenticeships, organised by stages. The Chambers of Handwork and Industry and Trade have involved their membership in a programme to extend this type of training to about 60% of 46,000 young people in the special schools who have little opportunity to obtain a regular apprenticeship (14). As one of the measures to combat the unemployment of young people, governments have sponsored additional, subsidized programmes in various training centres. France makes legal provision for entrance to apprenticeship for physically and mentally handicapped young people either through training in one of many centres specializing in aiding the handicapped or by a special contract between the employer, the apprentice, and one of the various government agencies which care for particular categories of handicapped and pay for the training and any extra expenses involved. Contracts for shorter periods of training may also be made in order to prepare the handicapped person for later entry to apprenticeship (15).

Young people who might leave school at the minimum leaving age with low academic credentials and enter unskilled work have been another target for recruitment to apprenticeship in some countries. The acceptance of such young people into apprenticeship has been an important source of increased numbers of apprentices in recent years in Austria and Switzerland, and in Germany has prevented a decline in the total number of apprentices (Appendix, Tables 2, 3, 4). Encouragement to low academic achievers to enter apprenticeship has been provided by the French pre-apprenticeship programme in which 14-year-olds can obtain some on-the-job experience in a firm at a nominal wage, continue their academic studies, and receive vocational skill training at an apprenticeship centre (CFA) at Ministry of Education expense. Preliminary results suggest that these young people perform better than some who enter apprenticeship at 16 years with the same background and qualifications. However, some reservations were expressed by French trainers about the least able and least motivated group which entered such craft trades as butchery. In Germany, the goal of 15% of apprenticeship places has been set for young people who leave compulsory school without a diploma. This figure includes the handicapped. Austrian trade unions are campaigning for apprenticeship status in certain semi-skilled training which such young people now enter. In Switzerland it has been urged that a shorter, more practical training with an examination only in the practical subjects, should be offered. Luxembourg has such a programme. In the United Kingdom programmes of vocational preparation for school-leavers who ordinarily enter jobs without training do not call for an expansion of the apprenticeship system, but rather for new efforts which may, in some cases, involve on-the-job training by employers. It is difficult in some countries to induce young people to enter apprenticeship since many young workers earn more than apprentices, and the gap between the earnings of skilled workers and semi-skilled and unskilled workers is narrowing. Earnings of apprentices vary greatly among occupations, and these differences, as well as differences in future earnings, influence the willingness to enter particular occupations.

The quantity and quality of apprenticeships vary greatly according to the size of a community, its degree of specialization, and its level of economic development. This has led to concern about young people who live in areas where apprenticeship opportunities are scarce or limited in type. Girls are particularly handicapped because of more limited mobility as well as the narrower range of choices they make, even when openings are more numerous and varied. In Germany, where apprenticeship is an important training method, the large, industrialized communities are seen as most favourable, but in France, where vocational education is more important than apprenticeship, the latter is said to be weakest in the economically advanced areas. In Germany analyses show clear regional differences in the unsatisfied demand for apprenticeship places and in the variety of training occupations available (16). As a part of the legislation of September 1976 to assure an adequate total number of apprenticeship places, the German government will be able to institute procedures to encourage the offer of apprenticeships in places where the unsatisfied demand for places is particularly high.

6. Employment after Apprenticeship

The traditional version of apprenticeship calls for employers or masters to try to retain all apprentices who sucessfully complete training. Today, a legal obligation to do so is rare. In Austria, employers may not discharge former apprentices during the three months after the completion of apprenticeship, and the trade unions are seeking an extension to six months. The actual facts about retention are, however, that one-third to one-half of the apprentices in many countries leave the training employer within the first year. Those who train in the smaller firms are more likely than others to make a change of firm. It appears that employers lose some apprentices they wish to retain because they find other jobs in which they may earn more, have more interesting work or discover other benefits. Employers also let a certain number of apprentices go because they are not needed as full-time employees or are not considered good enough workers. Such employers, who often have trained more apprentices than they can use, may end up hiring some apprentices trained by other employers because of the general reshuffle that occurs at the end of training (17). It is an oversimplification to think that the movement is only to employers who do not give training from those who do, although this is part of the complex picture.

In France, a survey carried out in 1976 by L'Assemblée Permanente des Chambres des Métiers revealed that: 89% of young people finishing apprenticeships in 1970 are in paid employment; 7% have set up in their own; 4% are seeking employment; 69% work in the branch for which they were trained or in a similar one; 89% are installed in the region where they trained; 71% started working life in the craft sector; 18% have taken further training. This survey, which covered

4,000 young people, does not however include any information on apprentices who have been taken on by the enterprise in which they were trained.

D. The Structure and Content of Training

The external regulation of apprenticeship training has developed because trainees are attached to individual employers whose ability and desire to provide satisfactory training cannot be taken for granted. All countries with an apprenticeship system have arrangements to ensure that apprenticeship training is planned and executed according to some agreed criteria. Regardless of the degree of government intervention, each country leaves a large measure of control over the apprenticeship system to the advisory or regulatory bodies on which employer and trade union representatives exercise an important or decisive influence. Ultimately, the approval of employers is essential, since their adverse reactions can lead to a diminution of apprenticeship openings.

The training regulations include provisions about the organisation and context of training, trade descriptions, training syllabuses, the duration of apprenticeship, provisions for complementary theoretical and general education, and the integration of the workplace and school components. Variations on these matters, both within and among countries, are the result of historical forces and traditional ways of doing things, differences in the perceived objectives and costs of training, divergent evaluations of the need for and benefits of the several elements of the training system, and the influences of particular political, social and economic circumstances. The duration of apprenticeship, for example, has tended to become shorter in recent years but there are still many differences among countries. In France most apprenticeships have been made into two-year programmes with the exception of some which involve artistic manual work. Many other countries with a range of two to four years tend to have a concentration of three-year programmes. However, the longer programmes in some of the English-speaking countries have only slowly been shortened. Employers have resisted it on the grounds that they would not recover their training costs in shorter periods, and trade unions have argued that the training would be inadequate, and that the wage structure for apprentices would be upset. It is not possible to define the optimum duration of an apprenticeship, nor is it clear how much variation there should be among trades, and how far the differences among countries represent real differences in the definitions of occupations and the content and level of training.

The assumption that all or most of the practical training will occur on the employer's premises is no longer valid. In several countries, apprenticeship systems have been modified so that a large proportion of all apprentices, and especially first-year apprentices, spend a fair amount of their training time away from their place of employment. Many firms are unable to provide a broad introduction to an occupation and a suitable range of practical training. This has led to establishment of a variety of alternatives and supplements: courses in educational institutions or group training centres, or training centres established by industrial training boards (United Kingdom), inter-occupational associations or other groups (France), intra-enterprise centres, and various types of training authorities (Germany), and AnCO centres in Ireland. In such centres and courses, training stages or modules can be used and the uniformity and level of training can be controlled and supervised more effectively than in individual firms. It is also possible to develop more satisfactory assessment systems.

In Germany, the Edding Commission directed its study of the costs and financing of apprenticeship to the quality of training. Applying an elaborate point system and ranking a large number of factors, the Commission established that apprenticeship training varied widely by size of firm, occupation, industry, and region. The quality of training ranked highest in areas of industrial concentration and was least satisfactory in predominantly rural areas. Although the law requires an individual training plan for each apprentice, such plans were lacking in 80% of the firms belonging to the Chambers of Handiwork, and in 32% of firms with fewer than 1,000 employees and 7.5% of those with 1,000 or more employees in the Chamber of Industry and Trade (33). While other countries have not examined the quality of their apprenticeship training as carefully or extensively, most are aware of the variations in it. The problem is to find remedies that will actually reduce the variability and bring the below-par trainers up to minimum standards. When policy also aims to maintain the number of available apprenticeships and to contain public expenditures the difficulties are magnified.

Theoretical and general education is an important part of apprenticeship. With the exception of enterprises that are capable of mounting their own educational programmes, or the French Centres de formation d'apprentissage (CFA), these courses are given by the educational system. Although the practice of releasing apprentices for this purpose is well established, some countries do not make it compulsory. In some countries the related instruction need not be given during working hours. However, most apprentices are released during working hours and given full pay or a living allowance for the time in education. Another way in which countries differ is in the content of the complementary education. The compulsory programmes in Austria, Switzerland and Germany offer a combination of general education and theoretical studies connected with the occupation. Where attendance is voluntary or under trade committee arrangements, the general education element is likely to be slight or non-existent. The traditional form of educational release which provided one day a week is being varied in some countries with "block" or "sandwich" release. Opinions vary about the time schedule for the educational segment. The nature and seasonality of the industry, the size of the firm, the way that the schools are organised, and the personal predilections of the trainers, teachers, and supervisors are important. While "block" release is the newer way of providing related education, and has distinct advantages it is by no means the universal choice.

In Austria, most apprentices attend separate schools, but in the United Kingdom the further educational and technical colleges cater to an assortment of students, as is also the case in Australia and parts of Germany. There are questions in most countries about the co-ordination of practical work and theoretical exercises. Particular problems have arisen in Germany where federal responsibility for training and state control over education hamper coordination, in spite of the efforts of federal-state commissions.

In some countries the quantity and quality of the teachers of general and theoretical education is an issue. The qualifications and experience of those who provide training in the practical areas are less standardized, on the whole, than those of the teachers giving related instruction in schools. The number of trainers and amount of time devoted to training is also likely to vary greatly with the size of the enterprise; the smaller firms are often at a disadvantage as far as the quantity, if not the quality of their trainers is concerned.

As a general rule training instructors must have a certain amount of experience as skilled workers; but it is less usual for their teaching ability to be tested carefully. Countries are in a better position in regard to instructors if an advanced certificate, such as Master Craftsman, is required of anyone training craft or artisan apprentices. Training courses and schools for instructors are becoming common in Britain and Ireland. In Germany it was decided in 1972 that uneven and inadequate training of apprentices was caused in part by short-comings in the preparation of either the training employer (Ausbildende) or the instructor (Ausbilder). A decree of April 1972 set new standards for employers and instructors who train in the industrial and commercial sectors, leaving the craft and artisan trainers to the provisions of their special Act of 1953. Strong reactions to the new high standards caused some modifications in July 1974, the chief effect being to reduce the number of existing instructors required to take the test. The government was however determined to maintain standards of competence for all instructors (18). Switzerland has introduced compulsory courses for trainers.

Many countries have established support institutions and personnel to ensure that the apprenticeship system will function as intended.

Advisers to firms, counsellors for apprentices, inspectors of health and safety provisions and other sources of aid have been created. It is difficult, however, to establish effectiveness of training in all the various occupations and among the firms of different sizes. Available information suggests that most countries have too few personnel with too many tasks in their inspection and supervisory services. If an annual visit is made to each training place this is a fairly good record. Another difficulty is that the policing of apprenticeship may be placed in the hands of agencies too closely associated with the employers. In Germany, where advisers both inspect training places and counsel apprentices, and where the Chambers which lay down the training regulations also employ and direct the advisers, a report notes that some counsellors are part-time or honorary. Moreover, counsellors are generally responsible for so many enterprises and trainees that many enterprises providing training cannot be visited regularly (19). A review of the situation in Ontario in 1973 observed that the apprenticeship counsellor whose task is to ensure that employers provide adequate practical instruction and conform to minimum standards is "in a very difficult position; to a large extent he is dependent upon the employer's good will and, if he takes the monitoring function too seriously, there is a high risk that the employer will refuse to participate in apprenticeship"(20). In Australia all apprenticeship authorities employ supervisors, but they have been so occupied with handling the complaints by employers and apprentices against each other that, according to the response to the OECD questionnaire, they have not had time to supervise the quality of training. Since 1972 apprentice training advisers, now numbering about 85, have been concentrating on upgrading the quality of training, but the official view is that their efforts do not nearly meet the needs of the situation. Whatever the faults of inspection and supervisory services, it is clear that the countries which have them and use them are in advance of those that rely on chance visits or complaints.

The representatives of Austrian labour have proposed that the adequacy of the training place should be determined before apprentices are hired, and that a licence should be issued to employers entitling them to offer training contracts. At present, the apprenticeship centres register apprenticeship contracts first and investigate employer's competence afterwards. In France, the law of 12th July 1971 maintains the basic principle of the employer's agreement but also aims to establish simpler methods for obtaining it in order to eliminate long waiting periods.

The establishment of vocational training research institutes and the financing of research in universities and other organisations is another important activity in the effort to improve the structure and content of training. The official German research institute has been developing training models which it hopes to disseminate widely, especially among the smaller firms without the personnel to develop such models for themselves.

E. Examination and Certification

In every country the completion of apprenticeship represents individual accomplishment and a potential for social, educational and economic advancement. However, the requirements for completion of an apprenticeship vary in many ways among OECD countries: whether the law or regulations provide for a final examination of the practical and theoretical achievements of apprentices; who prepares, administers and grades such examinations; what opportunities are provided for an apprentice who fails at the first attempt to be re-examined; whether certificates are awarded to those who complete apprenticeship; how acceptable such certificates are for mobility within and among countries; and how necessary certificates of completion are for entry into skilled jobs.

On the European continent, a legal requirement that apprentices take formal final examinations in order to achieve recognized completion is common. Intermediate examinations may be given in Switzerland. In France, the apprentices take the same examinations as vocational education students of the same age: they are set and graded by government authorities together with representatives of employers and trade unions. Elsewhere, the examinations are likely to be solely for apprentices and may be designed and graded by the semi-public or public bodies responsible for the training regulations. In Germany, where part-time theoretical studies are under the jurisdiction of the states, it is difficult to give standardized examinations, although efforts are being made to equalize and standardize the school component of apprenticeship throughout the country.

Among countries with no legislative provision for examinations, several variants are possible. Completion of apprenticeship may simply mean serving the required duration of the apprenticeship and attending the courses. Not only is there no statutory provision for practical and theoretical examinations, but there are no internally imposed final examinations either, although some apprentices may be given school tests in the theoretical subjects. Many apprenticeship trades in Australian states follow this pattern. In Britain the mix of apprenticeship regulation by collective agreement and the newer interventions of the industrial training boards tends increasingly to require some internal testing of practical accomplishments, especially at the end of off-the-job training. Apprentices usually elect to take the external City and Guilds examinations which test their theoretical knowledge, but this is not required in order to complete apprenticeship or receive recognition as a skilled worker. It is, however, helpful in order to progress to technician or return to further education. In Ireland until 1976 there were no compulsory examinations on the completion of apprenticeship and a number of apprentices did not take the examinations offered by the Department of Education in connection with block and day release studies. As AnCO staff put it in 1973: "Completion of the apprenticeship period is all that is required for recognition of skilled status, and membership of the appropriate union is deemed the hallmark of competence"(3). In 1975 the Council of AnCO declared that it accepted the principle of final testing and certification, but wished to see the details, including arrangements for continuous assessment and phase testing, completely worked out (4).

Data about the proportion of apprenticeships completed in a recent year (Table 3) indicate that formal examinations positively affect completion rates. However, several other factors are present which may in fact overshadow the role of examinations. They are affected by the average duration of apprenticeship, variations in the numbers entering from year to year, and the dropout rate. Taking all of these considerations into account, the data about completions (Table 3) suggest that formal examinations do not adversely affect the proportion of completions, and may indeed stimulate completion.

Countries with formal examination systems legally require an official certificate or diploma attesting to the successful completion of apprenticeship or an officially approved certificate issued by the enterprise. In Austria, an apprentice is entitled to receive a certificate of apprenticeship from the firm not only on completion, but also if the employer prematurely cancels the apprenticeship: the apprentice can obtain, on request, a pass or fail certificate for the examination, or a letter (Lehrbrief), certifying completion of the apprenticeship and examination success. Several countries where final examinations are given through the training bodies also provide by law for an official completion certificate. Such certificates may also be issued without final examinations, usually on request (United States, Ireland).

The issue of the geographical validity of apprenticeship certificates arises in federal countries where states regulate apprenticeship and in the Member countries of the EEC. The nine members of EEC have a project on the harmonization of training, including initial training which, in many countries, is largely provided by apprenticeship. Since the free movement of workers among Member countries is a principle of the EEC, it is likely that the countries whose population depends on emigration as a solution to domestic unemployment problems will wish to adjust their own training systems to conform to EEC regulations.

OECD countries differ markedly in the degree to which they observe legal or institutional provisions limiting access to skilled occupations to those who have satisfactorily completed an apprenticeship, either by

Table 3. APPRENTICESHIP COMPLETIONS

COUNTRY	YEAR	TOTAL NUMBER OF APPRENTICE-SHIPS	COMPLETIONS	COMPLETIONS AS % OF TOTAL NUMBER OF APPRENTICE-SHIPS
Austria [a]	1975	170,172	45,167	26.5
Australia	1975	131,899	26,183	19.9
Canada [b]	1974-75	67,070	10,030	15.0
France [a]	1975	200,000	–	–
Germany [a]	1975	1,328,906	536,108	40.5
Finland [a]	1975	2,744	835	30.4
Ireland	1975	15,000	–	–
New Zealand [c]	1976	29,420	5,619	19.0
Switzerland [a]	1975	145,904	47,201	32.4
United States	1976	254,968	49,650	19.5

NOTES:
a) Government authorized formal examinations required.
b) Data exclude Quebec. Some provinces have formal examinations.
c) Private sector only.

SOURCE: National statistics.

passing examinations or serving time. Three groups of countries may be distinguished in this connection: the continental European nations; the United Kingdom, and some of the countries which inherited the British apprenticeship system (Ireland, Australia); and the North American countries.

In the continental European countries where apprenticeship and its credentials are widely accepted skilled work may be performed by anyone an employer chooses to do the job. Skilled jobs are not reserved either by law or institutional arrangement for those who possess an apprenticeship certificate or other occupational training certificate. Trade unions do not insist on limiting access either to their own members or to those who have completed apprenticeship in a specific craft. However, the young people who furnish the skilled labour force for the apprenticeable occupations in Germany, Austria and Switzerland are so likely to complete an apprenticeship that in fact a very high proportion of skilled workers have come through the apprenticeship route. A study in Germany in 1970 found that 90% of all male skilled workers had completed an apprenticeship, but not necessarily in the occupation in which they were employed. A similar British inquiry among craftsmen employed in the engineering industries discovered that 80% had completed an apprenticeship, but it may be assumed that almost all were employed in the particular craft occupation in which the apprenticeship had been completed (9).

The apprenticeship system in Britain relates more directly to specific employment possibilities than it does in Germany. In Germany, where offers of employers are not planned and do not attempt to correspond to the needs of the labour market, a recent study found marked discrepancies between the occupational distribution of the labour force and the distribution of apprenticeship occupations (24). On the assumption that apprenticeship training is economically wasteful if imbalances force many apprentices to change their occupations when they seek jobs, the study calculated the deficits and surpluses in male apprenticeship places in 1970 according to the distribution of the skilled male labour force. Among the fields with heavy surpluses were some that apprentices favour particularly: mechanics, locksmiths and fitters. While almost half of all apprentice trainees were in the craft or artisan trades, only 19% of the skilled labour force was employed in this sector in 1970. The study concluded that fairly easy occupational mobility as a result of severe labour scarcities had saved the situation. However, the element of substitution in employment for those who have completed an apprenticeship is also potentially greater in Germany than in the English-speaking countries.

American trade unions are not as dedicated to apprenticeship as those in some other English-speaking countries where apprenticeship is the chief method of acquiring skill. The deputy administrator of the US Department of Labour Bureau of Apprenticeship Training, noted that union limitations on the expansion of apprenticeship have arisen because "industrial unions are concerned lest the apprenticeship system disturb seniority rights of workers and limit entrance into the skilled crafts lines to a single method. Many unions want to continue to accept anyone who is 'qualified' and to retain the right to decide what qualified means in terms of the local labour market. Unions, and to a lesser extent employers, recognize demands of peak periods and will not restrict achievement of journeyman status only to completing apprentices" (10). In the building trades, which account for more than a half of all American apprenticeships, a majority of qualified craftsmen have had apprenticeship training but only a small minority of them have completed training. Trade unions award union cards to those with "part of the trade" and utilize safety valve mechanisms such as temporary permits and travellers' cards (25).

F. Financing of Apprenticeship

   1. Employer Responsibility

Traditionally, the cost of training apprentices has been borne by individual employers or, in a few countries, by joint employer/trade union committees or by trade unions alone. The private sponsors have been expected to bear all the costs connected with training in the enterprise. Among the special costs which employers or sponsors bear in some countries are the fees for taking the craftsman's test, health insurance, apprentices' tools, and, in Denmark, compensation to an apprentice who fails a test because the employer does not provide the training certified in the contract. The administrative costs of the Chambers or other bodies with day-to-day responsibility for apprenticeship programmes usually fall entirely or in large part on those who employ the apprentices. Beside the wages or allowances paid for the time spent on the job, apprentices in many countries must be paid by the employer for the time spent at schools for general or related theoretical education. Almost everywhere the costs of the school component have been entirely or largely borne by governments as part of the education system, although employers in some countries have paid school fees for apprentices. Under various arrangements for joint training centres, employers may be required by legislation or agreements to make financial contributions to such centres whose activities may entirely or partially offset training costs within the enterprise. The rationale for having the individual employer bear the costs of apprenticeship training is found in three sets of circumstances in the traditional apprenticeship situation. First, most of the employers within an occupation offered apprenticeship training. Second, the period of apprenticeship was long enough for the employer to recoup his costs of training and register a profit from the apprentice's contribution to production. Third, apprentices did not leave during apprenticeship and remained with the employer afterwards. Currently, all three conditions have changed in many countries for a substantial portion of employers who offer or who might offer training.

   a) How many employers train apprentices?

Only a few countries have been able to determine the percentage of employers offering apprenticeships because data are lacking about the total number of them which should form the base for such a calculation. But there has been a general awareness in countries where apprenticeship is an important route to skilled status that only a fraction of the relevant employers do train apprentices. A survey of training-in-industry in Ontario in 1968-69 showed that 12.7% of the enterprise responding were involved in apprenticeship (20). Evidence for Germany indicates that the proportion of relevant enterprises offering apprenticeship posts is not large, has been declining, and varies according to the size of the enterprise, the type of occupation, and to the economic position of the enterprise, industry and economy. The Edding Commission estimated in 1972-73 that about one-fourth of the artisan and craft (Handwerk) enterprises and one-tenth of those in industry and trade (Industrie und Handel) offered apprenticeship training (33). Since these calculations include one-person and one-employee enterprises, small family enterprises, those not authorized to train and those which need no skilled workers trained through apprenticeship, they overstate the total number of relevant enterprises and understate the proportion which offer apprenticeship.

The distribution of apprenticeship training among enterprises according to the size of establishment, has been of considerable recent interest because of its implications for financing. Data from several sources on training enterprises in Germany is classified according to the number of employees (Table 4). Columns 1 and 2 refer to a sample study at the end of 1975 covering seven of the 73 local Chambers of Industry and Commerce and encompassing 172,288 employers, of whom 97,776 were listed without being assigned to a size-class. The larger the size-of-firm class, measured by number of employees, the higher the proportion of firms offering one or more apprenticeships (column 1). The progression of percentage is steady, from 2.9% of the unclassified firms (many of which are probably one-man or family enterprises dealing in consumer services or small shops or kiosks selling newspapers and similar items) to 84.8% of firms with 1,000 employees or more, most of which are no doubt industrial. On average, only 8.1% of all firms offered one or more apprenticeships in 1975. The proportion of all apprenticeships provided by each size-class is not regular, although over half of all apprentices are in firms with 50 or more workers (column 2). The necessary base figures of the total employment in these firms are lacking. However, the deficiency is remedied in a national sample study in 1970 of apprenticeships in all fields covered by the law, not just in industry and trade (columns 3, 4, 5). The tendency of the smaller-size firms, especially in handicrafts, to train disproportionately to their total number of employees appears clearly. In 1970, firms employing under 50 persons trained 57.3% of all apprentices, but employed only 43.6% of all employees. The small firms seem to be less likely to offer apprenticeship than the large, but among firms which do offer apprenticeship, a higher proportion of all apprentices are trained in small than in large firms. Thus the uneven sharing of training costs among employers is more marked for the smaller than the larger sized firms. If apprentices trained in small firms gravitate toward larger firms, as seems to be the case, the smaller firms which have done no training may benefit little from the heavy training done by others, and large firms may reap the benefits. This record has been interpreted by policy-makers and others in such a way as to show that the larger German firms are not

Table 4. TRAINING FIRMS AND APPRENTICES, BY SIZE OF FIRM, GERMANY

NUMBER OF EMPLOYEES	FIRMS WITH APPRENTICES AS % OF ALL FIRMS IN SIZE CLASS	DISTRIBUTION OF APPRENTICES (%)	APPRENTICES PER 100 EMPLOYEES	DISTRIBUTION OF TOTAL EMPLOYMENT (%)	DISTRIBUTION OF APPRENTICES (%)	DISTRIBUTION OF TOTAL EMPLOYMENT IN ARTISAN TRADES (%)
	1	2	3	4	5	6
Unknown	2.9	13.3				
1 - 4	-	-	10.5	13.3	10.3	20.5
5 - 9	-	-	13.4	9.5	19.2	22.1
Under 10	6.8	9.0	-	-	-	-
10 - 19	27.3	5.1	9.4	8.5	14.0	15.5
20 - 49	37.0	8.1	6.1	12.3	13.8	17.8
50 - 99	46.1	8.0	4.8	9.8	8.8	
100 - 199	58.0	9.2	4.4	9.8	8.2	
200 - 499	67.9	13.0	4.0	12.6	9.7	24.1
500 - 999	78.1	9.3	} 3.5	} 24.2	} 16.0	
1,000 and over	84.8	25.1				
TOTAL	8.1	100.0	5.9	100.0	100.0	100.0

NOTES: Columns 1 and 2. Data from sample survey of seven local Chambers of Industry and Trade, 1975 Columns 3, 4 and 5. Data from national sample survey, 1970.

SOURCES: Columns 1 and 2 Deutscher Industrie- und Handelstag. Berufsbildung 1975/76, pp. 60-61. 1975 data.
Column 3. Unpublished data from the Ministry of Education and Science (BMBW). 1970 data.
Columns 4 and 5. Ministry of Education and Science. Bildungspolitische Zwischenbilanz, Bonn, 1976, p. 16. 1970 data.
Column 6. Zentralverband des Deutschen Handwerks. Bonn, 1976. 1975 data.

training adequate numbers and must be stimulated to better performance (26). On the other hand, the record has also been interpreted as evidence that the small firms, particularly in artisan and crafts occupations, have been training a surplus over their own as well as the occupation's current need for skilled manpower. This excess causes numerous occupational shifts by apprentices on completing training and produces a mismatch between the training supply and labour force requirements (20, 27).

Information in Britain about employer training by size of firm supports the findings in Germany. On one hand, relatively fewer small firms are said to offer apprenticeships. On the other, the small manufacturing firms with 11 to 249 employees have a higher proportion of apprentices in relation to their total employment than the other two size classes (Table 5). The small British manufacturing firms have had higher percentages of apprentices than the medium or large firms in more than half of the industries for which detailed data are available. In only a few British industries, however, has the absolute number of apprentices been larger in the small firms than in the medium or large firms (28). There is also indirect evidence that the smallest firms, employing the highest proportion of craftsmen, lose many who have served apprenticeships with them, since they report the greatest shortages of skilled workers (29).

 b) Training costs

Many firms that employ skilled workers do not bear appropriate costs of training because they train no apprentices at all or train at lower levels than are required to meet their own recruitment needs. One cause of their reluctance has been the steadily increasing costs of training apprentices compared with their contribution to output. The belief that apprenticeship had become less profitable was voiced in the early 1960s in regard to the artisan trades in Germany (30). In response to an OECD questionnaire in 1976, Switzerland submitted a report on costs in Zurich. Employers say that the rising level of training costs may lead them to abandon or reduce apprenticeship training, and list the following factors that have raised employers' training costs compared with apprentices' contributions to production: social legislation and collective agreements, which have reduced the number of hours devoted to production, longer paid vacations, longer periods of theoretical study, and the introduction of intra-firm training centres which take apprentices away from production. In addition, the experience of several countries indicates that the following factors tend to raise costs without a corresponding increase in apprentice output: higher taxes for social benefits, the prolongation of compulsory education, the higher costs for trainers because of new standards imposed by law, shorter duration of apprenticeships, higher turnover rates of apprentices during and at the end of training, more stringent

Table 5. EMPLOYMENT AND TRAINING IN MANUFACTURING INDUSTRIES, BY SIZE OF FIRM, GREAT BRITAIN, 1968

	11-249 EMPLOYEES		250-499 EMPLOYEES		500 OR MORE EMPLOYEES		ALL FIRMS 11 EMPLOYEES AND OVER	
	NUMBER OF EMPLOYEES	%		%		%	NUMBER OF EMPLOYEES	%
Total employment..	2,786,490	35.0	1,143,960	14.4	4,026,352	50.6	7,956,802	100.0
Apprentices.	91,360	38.7	24,730	10.5	119,920	50.8	236,010	100.0
Others in training								
Under 18 ..	40,630	52.4	11,940	15.4	24,970	32.2	77,540	100.0
18 and over	49,800	38.1	18,670	14.3	62,280	47.6	130,750	100.0

SOURCE: Employment and Productivity Gazette, January 1969, p. 35.

minimum standards for premises, equipment and safety, and increased wage rates for apprentices compared with both skilled workers and unskilled youth.

Minimum wage rates payable to apprentices are lowest in the first year of apprenticeship and increase at intervals with the highest rates reached in the final year. Reductions in the duration of apprenticeships result in more rapid increases in wages. In recent years starting rates for apprentices, expressed as a percentage of minimum or prevailing rates for skilled workers, have tended to rise, and rates in the final year have tended to come close to the craftsman's rate, partly as a result of the trend toward paying adult wage rates to young workers at 18 instead of 21 (Appendix, Table 12). Actual rates of pay often exceed prescribed minima and in some countries it is possible for apprentices to obtain the craftsman's rate before the end of formal training. Occupational differences in apprentice pay are marked within countries (Appendix, Table 12). The Edding Commission noted that wage costs constituted almost half of the total costs of German apprenticeship. This is in marked contrast to the earlier situation when apprentices received small allowances to cover out-of-pocket expenses (33). A study published in 1966 states that a 15-to-16-year-old apprentice in European countries where apprenticeship was strong might receive as little as 10% of a journeyman's wage (30), but now it is rare to find apprentices starting at less than 30-40% of the skilled rate.

Another way in which apprentices may become more costly to an enterprise is through changes in technology or organisation. In Germany, research has been most explicit in revealing the adverse effects on the costs and convenience of offering training when enterprises adopt more automated techniques and sometimes need fewer skilled workers (31).

The costs to employers of apprenticeship training have been calculated in only a few countries. There is even less material on the total costs of apprenticeship training, including the school component for theoretical or general education (32, 33). Still fewer studies are available about the cost-effectiveness of apprenticeship training in comparison with other methods of instilling occupational skills, or about their costs and benefits to employers, apprentices and society (34).

By far the most ambitious attempt to study the costs of apprenticeship has been that of the Edding Commission in Germany. It investigated the training costs of enterprises (including public enterprises, such as the postal service and railways) which differed by type, size and geographical location in a variety of occupations and industries. Confining itself to the training offered by employers in practical skills, the Commission constructed its own method for measuring direct and indirect gross and net costs. Its report, delivered in 1974 after three years' work, established that the gross yearly expenditure on training each apprentice varied from DM. 86 in health occupations to DM. 8,912 in firms with 1,000 or more employees belonging to the Chambers of Industry and Commerce. A much wider range was found when individual firms were considered, with some spending as much as DM. 22,000 a year on training a commercial apprentice. Net cost estimates demonstrated that only 10.4% of the firms sampled made a profit or broke even on apprenticeship training and that such firms were disproportionately found among members of the Chambers of Handiwork. About 30% of all firms had net costs of DM. 1,000 to DM. 2,500 a year per apprentice, while 6.7% had costs in excess of DM. 10,000 (33).

A report based on an investigation in 1973 in Ontario stated that "the available evidence strongly suggests that complete reliance on the traditional wage mechanism to finance on-the-job instruction for apprentices is no longer practical" (20). This conclusion was based on evidence that employers often "refuse to enter into a contract of apprenticeship because they believe it is too costly" or they consider it "a high risk proposition", since "apprentices are free to leave during training". In the United Kingdom, during preparatory discussions of the Industrial Training Act of 1964, the same points were made (36). In connection with its evaluation of the quality of initial vocational training in Germany, the Edding Commission concluded that deficiencies in quality could only be remedied if there were changes in the system of financing apprenticeship so as not to rely on individual employers. In several countries moves to change the method of financing have stemmed from concern about the quality of training, the uneven distribution of the training effort among employers, and conjunctural and secular shortfalls in total apprenticeship intake in some countries.

c) Conjunctural and secular influences on intake

One of the most serious policy issues of apprenticeship as an integral part of the training and educational system of a country is its instability during the business cycle. Since apprenticeship is essentially an employment relationship, employers are guided by general employment and business conditions as well as their own specific situation and expectations in deciding how many apprentices to recruit and retain. During recessions these numbers decline along with employment as a whole, and the diminished numbers in training serve as a brake on later expansion because of the lag between beginning and completing apprenticeship. Various countries have documented the existence of cycles of apprenticeship intake and total numbers.

In the United Kingdom apprenticeship openings, the intake of new apprentices, and the total number of apprentices all fluctuate conjuncturally. The pattern of fluctuations in the index of all apprentices in training is similar to the pattern for all skilled workers, a good indicator of general business conditions. In Australia relatively low unemployment rates and a high rate of economic growth until very recently deflected interest from conjunctural fluctuations in apprenticeship intake or numbers. Recent research on the Australian building industry, however, indicates that intake of new apprentices declines as unemployment in that industry rises. In the United States the number of new apprentices registered appears to be inversely related to annual average unemployment, while the apprentice completion rate, which also fluctuates conjuncturally, is directly related to annual average unemployment. In Canada, as in the United States, there appears to be an inverse correlation between new apprenticeship registrations and unemployment rates (20).

In Germany, where employment has been high in most years since the early 1950s, the usual situation has been a large surplus of unfilled apprenticeship openings. Conjunctural fluctuations have occurred, however, in the proportion of all apprentices employed by firms belonging to the Chambers of Industry and Commerce, and in the proportion employed by firms in the Chambers of Handiwork (33). Would-be apprentices prefer employment in the more advanced sector of the economy (i.e., firms and occupations included in the Chambers of Industry and Commerce). As the firms with higher training costs and better quality of training retrench in recession, a larger number and proportion of would-be apprentices accept openings in firms in the artisan trades, which usually have a large proportion of unfilled openings in good years. The proportion of all apprentices in firms belonging to the Chambers of Industry and Commerce thus fluctuates with the fluctuations of other relevant economic indicators. A particularly close relationship exists between rates of growth of industrial investment and the proportion of all apprentices under the jurisdiction of the Chambers of Industry and Commerce when the proportion of apprentices is lagged by one year.

Another source of distortion between the numbers trained through apprenticeship and the numbers of skilled workers required by the economy arises from the adverse effects of technological and organisational changes on employers' willingness to train apprentices in the advanced industrial and commercial sectors. Some employers who reduce or eliminate apprenticeship because of these changes continue to hire away the apprentices trained by other employers. This issue is important only in the countries where apprenticeship has historically been important in these sectors. Several countries have discovered that the changing structure, technology and organisation of certain industries have reduced the demand for apprentices over time. In some countries the diminution is relative rather than absolute and it may be concealed because other sectors of the economy have increased their total demand for apprentices or have been able to fill vacancies that previously were open. The analysis of secular changes examines specific industries and also changes in the composition of apprenticeship by occupational categories. Research is in an early stage and is less developed than inquiries into conjunctural effects. In fact, some secular movements are concealed or mis-read as conjunctural disturbances, and vice versa. The British engineering industries and shipbuilding, among the largest employers of apprentices, have experienced a decline both in the proportion that craftsmen constitute of total employment and in the ratio of apprentices to craftsmen. According to employers, a fair number of workers designated as craftsmen because of trade union pressures to maintain status and wages actually perform semi-skilled work, further reducing the share of actual craftsmen in the industry's labour force (37).

Studies in Germany have attempted to measure the changes from 1962 to 1972 in the intensity of apprenticeship training in industrial firms covered by the Chambers of Industry and Trade, distinguishing between blue-collar and white-collar occupations (31). The main findings were as follows:

    i) The relative ranking of industries according to the intensity of their training activities (the ratio of skilled workers to apprentices) hardly changed over the decade. A wide range persists in training ratios for skilled workers. In 1972, at the upper end there were about 5 skilled workers to each apprentice in the electrical goods industry, and at the other end a ratio of about 200:1 in the tobacco industry.

    ii) From 1962 to 1972 a decline in training activities occurred in most industries, with the reduction particularly marked in the industries which had the highest training intensity in 1962.

    iii) Reductions in training intensity in blue-collar occupations were the result of a diminished need for skilled workers. In white-collar occupations, however, it was because training failed to increase as rapidly as employment.

    iv) Over the decade 1962-72, the training efforts of firms changed differently according to their size and the particular industry concerned. In some industries the growing size of establishments was associated with a decline of the training intensity. In other industries the larger establishments increased their training intensity, while below a certain size-class the intensity decreased over the decade.

A regression analysis from the same data suggested that the training decisions of firms were chiefly influenced by changes in the demand for skilled workers due to mechanization, organisational changes, and changes in the size of establishment, and increased difficulties in offering training which conforms to the apprenticeship regulations. Data from the employment service on the proportion of school-leavers who requested assistance in finding an apprenticeship opening showed a slightly rising trend from 1962 to 1970 and then a drop to 1972. This variable had a negative, but not statistically significant impact on the total number of apprentices.

2. Collective Financing

In the United States collective financing takes the form of a pooling of voluntary contributions from employers and trade unions in one or more training funds, which are then redistributed to pay for training. In the United Kingdom collective financing was initiated by the Industrial Training Act of 1964. Commonly called the levy-grant system, such a measure was considered and rejected by Ontario, Canada, but was enacted in 1967 in Ireland. In 1971 France instituted its own version, and in Germany under legislation effective in September 1976 a levy-grant may be activated under certain conditions on a year-to-year basis. In 1973, the United Kingdom added a new element: financial contributions from government.

The 1964 Industrial Training Act in the United Kingdom was not directed specifically toward apprenticeship, but covered every type of training from operatives to management. However, the training of apprentices to skilled worker level has been the major activity of most Industrial Training Boards. As described by the Manpower Services Commission, the outcomes of the 1964 Act were disappointing. Although the Industrial Training Boards have secured real improvements in the quality of training, the system did not succeed in raising the quantity of transferable skill training to the level required to meet the needs of industry generally. The fundamental reason for the inadequacy of the 1964 Act in this respect was that although it provided a mechanism for relieving the individual employers of at least part of the cost of training, which influences employers' decisions about levels of recruitment, it did not provide a means by which the Training Boards could ensure that overall levels of recruitment into an industry were sufficient to meet the industry's long-term needs (38). Other evaluations have suggested that the system was inadequate because it was based on a financial incentive alone, ignoring the other factors which influence training decisions by management and the doubts of employers and the Boards about the effects of the system in stimulating training (39).

When discussions of proposed changes in the 1964 Act began in 1972, the phasing out of the levy-grant system and a return to individual financing by employers was debated. The amendments incorporated in the Employment and Training Act of 1973 replaced the former system by a system of levy-grant and exemptions. They also provided that the newly created, quasi-public Manpower Services Commission, through its Training Services Agency, should pay the administrative and operating expenses of the Training Boards. Dissatisfaction with the results of the 1973 amendments led the Department of Employment and the Manpower Services Commission in July 1976 to put forward a new financing idea, called "collective funding", on which a wide range of organisations and individuals were invited to comment. The discussion document described a fund, jointly financed by government and employers, which would exist alongside a modified version of the existing levy-grant-exemption system. It would pay for all or a large part of initial training in the wider-based or transferable skills. The document gave strong support to apprenticeship as the primary method of training for transferable skills, despite its shortcomings in providing the economy with an adequate supply (38).

The main reasons given for the shortfall in training intake were the dampening effects of recession and the expenses of training which made some employers content to poach skilled labour from other employers at all times. A plan was proposed whereby industry, government and the Manpower Services Commission would prepare a list of skills that are transferable from one employer and from one industry to another, and which are so vital to the economy as to require special measures to ensure a proper supply of initial trainees. Each year recruitment targets would be set, according to the long-term needs of industry. Using the Training Boards or individual employers in fields without a training board, contracts would be signed for adequate levels of training. If employers did not take on sufficient numbers of young people for training, the Boards could recruit them and provide off-the-job training. In essence, first-year training was to be financed in this way, leaving later training for employers to finance. Because first-year training might be largely off-the-job, employers would recover little in productive work and therefore the gross training costs would be the basis for reimbursement. Small firms, currently exempt from the levy but eligible for a grant, might continue in this position under the proposed scheme because they do some transferable skill training. The actual cost of the fund to employers would be not more than 0.25% of the wage-bill and the practical proposals for the division of training costs between public and private sources ranged from 50/50 to 30/70, depending somewhat on the percentage of the employers' training costs to be reimbursed. The document proposed that the Boards' operating costs be financed entirely from a levy, freeing public funds for the direct financing of training (35, 38).

The public discussion was conducted in a period when serious attempts were being made to curtail government expenditures, and there were doubts about the possibility of obtaining substantial public contributions to a collective fund. But there were adverse reactions for other reasons. A Task Group, including representatives from trade unions, employers, Industrial Training Boards, the education service and officials of the TSA was established under the Chairman of the Manpower Services Commission and was asked to present proposals "for action which would help to ease problems arising from skill shortages", paying particular attention to training measures, financial mechanisms and resources, and the systematic recruitment of young people.

The report was published in mid-1977 and concluded that the principal responsibility for securing training and related further education lies with industry itself, assisted by the Industrial Training Boards and similar organisations. Intervention by the Manpower Services Commission was approved for key areas only, where the desired results would not otherwise be achieved (40). The MSC could be most helpful where training activities were common to a number of occupations and coordination was required: where ITBs and other national organisations believe that they cannot succeed without additional resources; where training is in skills that are important from a national viewpoint, and where the industries are shouldering the main burden themselves. The MSC was urged to discontinue its funding of special measures for one year at a time and, instead, to obtain sufficient funds from Government to maintain a consistent and permanent means to deal with training in important skills (40). The special measures would end with the intakes for 1978-79 and the new programmes would then be based on rolling five-year strategic reviews.

In France there is a general apprenticeship tax on employers, but before 1971 (when it was 0.6% of the wage-bill) collections were poorly enforced and the receipts were applied only partially to apprenticeship and vocational training. The 1971 law and subsequent implementing decrees to improve the quality of apprenticeship provided for the establishment of the Centres de formation d'apprentis (CFA) to offer both off-the-job practical training and theoretical and general education. In order to finance the CFA and cover other costs, the receipts from the apprenticeship tax, now set at 0.5% of the wage-bill, are specifically allocated so that a fixed quota (20% in 1977) is reserved for apprenticeship. In addition, other portions of the receipts of the apprenticeship tax are used to finance apprenticeship and pre-apprenticeship. In 1975, the tax yield was about Frs. 1,700 million, of which apprenticeship received Frs. 871 million. Receipts from the tax are affected by the provision that employers may deduct from their tax obligation a variety of training expenditures they make. Other types of vocational training absorb the balance of the tax receipts not spent on apprenticeship. While employers who do not train must contribute toward a fund used to foster apprenticeship, the fund does not subsidize employers for their in-plant training costs, with the exception of the payments made to firms in the artisan and commercial trades which accept pre-apprentices. Tax receipts may also be used to recompense employers for the wages and other costs for apprentices while they attend the CFA. The law of 12th July 1977 provides for a subsidy towards training costs for training on the premises for employers with less than 10 employees. The amount of the subsidy will be reviewed annually.

In Germany, the final report of the Edding Commission stated that a reform of the system of financing was a precondition of any reform of vocational training. The Commission proposed that a central fund should replace individual financing by employers, and that all employers, whether they train or not, should pay a levy of 1% of the wage-bill in order to finance apprenticeship. Firms which offer apprenticeship training of the required quality would be reimbursed full standard costs; and those which gave training of superior quality would get extra payments. At the same time attempts would be made to rationalize costs. The advantages of a central fund, as described by the Commission, are that it helps eliminate competitive disadvantages between those who train and those who do not, that it can set up information and advisory services for apprentices and their parents, that it can ameliorate regional inequalities and provide more regular intake during fluctuations in activity. In particular, it can improve the training opportunities for retarded and handicapped juveniles (16). The measure signed into law in September 1976 was not the central fund recommended by the Edding Commission, but rather a more limited provision. The new law (Ausbildungsplatzförderungsgesetz) provides for a yearly calculation of the number of apprenticeships desired by young people and the number of vacancies offered by employers. In any year when it appears that the vacancies will not exceed the demand for places by at least 12.5%, the government may levy a payroll tax of not over 0.25% on all firms whose annual business turnover exceeds DM. 400,000. The purpose is to exempt firms with fewer than 20 employees, and the estimate is that under these provisions, 90% of all enterprises would be exempt. The fund thus created can finance subsidies to enterprises which create additional training places over and above their average number for the previous three years. Firms which add apprentices during the calendar year when the statute comes into effect can obtain grants, without regard to their previous record, if they do not qualify under the first provision. If the grants provided in the first two categories are not adequate to maintain training places which are in danger of being eliminated, special aid can be given with a view to attaining a balance between supply and demand at the regional level and for intra-firm training centres.

Questions of principle and practice have brought this new law under heavy criticism from employers. Maintaining that employers will provide an adequate number of places without government interference of this kind, some group of employers expressed preferences for tax credits or outright grants to those who train, rather than subsidies paid from a payroll tax. The concentration of the tax on the 10% of large firms was cited as inequitable and a waste of time, since the taxes would merely recirculate to those who had paid them. On the practical side, the decision on when to institute the tax will be difficult to make, given the unreliability of data about the supply of and demand for places. Moreover, if the tax is levied and there are surplus places in some areas or in some occupations, there will be complaints, even if some young people are not placed. Nor is there any guarantee that the new apprenticeship places created through the fund will correspond to the residence and occupational choices of the would-be apprentices. Some employers maintain that the subsidies may go to the firms which had reduced their training places earlier, penalizing those which maintained or increased them in the face of business reverses. The distinctive feature of the German measure is that it provides a vehicle for government intervention, not only under conditions but also in periods when the number of young people is rising, as it will until the early 1980s, because of demographic factors. Collective financing, in this case, is called upon to absorb young people without regard to the immediate need for their skills, but as a stockpiling effort to provide skilled workers for a decade ahead. Since the response of employers to the threat of a tax has been to increase the number of new apprenticeships offered for 1977 and 1978, tax has not yet been levied.

3. Government Financial Assistance to Employers

Parallel to the government initiatives to spread the costs of training more evenly among firms which train apprentices and firms which do not, efforts have been made to provide public financial relief and incentives to training firms. In part, such financial assistance from government has been motivated by the desire to increase the intake of apprentices, but it also aims at improving the quality of training and shortening the duration of training. In announcing a new financial support scheme for apprenticeship in Australia, the Ministers stated that the programme "acknowledges that the community should support the technical costs of apprentice training as it supports education for the professions and sub-professional occupations".

Governmental financial aid programmes may be either permanent or temporary, or variable in response to changes in economic conditions. Among the permanent programmes are arrangements to deduct all training costs of the enterprise from taxable operating profits. In several countries, employers are not obliged to pay their apprentices' wages for the time they spend in related theoretical and general education. Either the employer is reimbursed or the apprentice is paid directly. The payment may be lower than the ordinary apprentice wage, as in the case of Canada, where the Federal Goverment provides funds for the payment of income support in addition to the payment of costs of theoretical instruction provided in training institutions. The cost of such training allowances to apprentices in Ontario in the period 1969-1972 came to roughly two-thirds the cost of providing the related education (20).

In France, the National Employment Pact for Young People (July 1977) stipulates that new contracts taken up between 1st July and 31st December 1977 will be exempt from employers' social security contributions for the whole length of the contract. This measure had considerable effect, since 82,200 apprenticeship places benefited from this exemption by December 1977. In a normal year about 60,000 apprentices are taken on.

The new programme Commonwealth Rebate for Apprentice Full-time Training (CRAFT) in Australia offers a tax-exempt subsidy to employers for all apprentices taken on after January 1977. The rebate is paid at a fixed daily amount for every full day of release time that apprentices are granted by employers in order to attend (or study through correspondence) a basic technical education course, prescribed by a state or territory apprenticeship authority. In addition, a tax-exempt subsidy will be paid to employers for permitting attendance at off-the-job training courses, which supplement basic trade courses. Payments can be made for up to 130 days in the second and third years of apprenticeship and are dependent on completion of a stage of the course. Such courses may be carried out in a training area, separate from production, in the employer's own establishment, or in another training centre. Courses must be approved by the regional office of the federal Department of Employment and Industrial Relations. An employer with spare training space can also qualify for additional grants if he acts as "host trainer" to the apprentices of other employers and offers approved training courses. Moreover, a group of employers who come together to form a training centre can receive additional sums besides the tax-exempt subsidy for each apprentice's released time.

In Finland the law of 1967, amended in 1973, provides employers with a monthly subsidy for each apprentice who has worked for them for at least 14 days a month. The amounts vary, and are larger for the first year of apprenticeship than the subsequent years. The Netherlands have long subsidized the Foundations which operate apprenticeship.

In July 1977 France introduced a two-year programme to relieve employers of the cost of social security contributions for newly hired apprentices in the period July-December 1977. Special financial assistance was offered to craftsmen and small businesses that took on additional apprentices. The average cost of the measure is estimated to be Frs. 1,400 per year for each eligible apprentice.

In the United States, where in principle the financing of apprenticeship is the responsibility of the private sector, federal government assistance was first granted in response to the federal emphasis on opening apprenticeship to minority groups. Comprehensive Employment and Training Act (CETA) funds have supported a variety of apprenticeship activities, such as apprenticeship instructors, salaries of co-ordinators, secretaries, and other administrative personnel; apprenticeship and training representatives; recruitment, remedial education, tutoring, counselling; the development of an automated apprentice information system; and reimbursements to employers for training costs, direct stipends to apprentices, bookkeeping services, instructional equipment, and itinerant instruction in rural areas. Funding ranges from a few thousand dollars to several million (10). Supplementing the federal funds allotted to the extension and improvement of apprenticeship the United States government has added federally financed experimental initiatives and other programmes (41). An indirect wage subsidy is paid through the provision that the education and training allowances to veterans include apprenticeship. Since 45% of apprentices in 1974 were veterans and 75% of these veterans were in receipt of education allowances or on-the-job training allowances, a substantial financial underpinning of the wage structure was furnished by the government (42).

In Australia a pre-apprenticeship or pre-vocational programme has been launched. It is explicitly structured so that the total duration of apprenticeship can be reduced from four to three years with little loss to the employer of productive time. Young people entering these programmes are paid allowances by the government, although they are actually in full-time attendance at a technical school which others may attend without allowances. Payment of such pre-apprentices for study is easier in countries which also pay allowances to young people in full-time education.

Another type of indirect assistance to employers has been the financial contributions by the German Government to the construction and furnishing of places in inter-firm branch training centres for the industries and occupations which consist mainly of small firms whose facilities are inadequate to offer the full range of training required by the regulations for apprenticeship training. The funds are used as incentives to build such centres, which remain institutions of the trade associations or groups of associations. Such centres had 23,000 training places in 1973 and 77,000 are planned by 1981.

Seven different measures to bolster craft apprenticeship through financial support from the Training Services Agency were devised in the United Kingdom as a recession programme (43) intended to meet future shortfalls and to safeguard the continuity of the individual's training. The programme is expected to last until May 1980.

i) <u>Premium grants (off-the-job)</u>. A grant of £2,000 for 12 months is paid to employers for each trainee in excess of normal intake who is taken on for at least two years of training, is guaranteed a complete apprenticeship, and will receive initial training off-the-job, including associated further education.

ii) <u>Premium grants (on-the-job)</u>. A grant of up to £850 is available under the same conditions to employers for approximately one year of on-the-job training in apprenticeable occupations. From July 1975 to July 1977 some 30,000 grants were made for off-the-job and on-the-job premium grants.

iii) <u>Training awards</u>. Training is given under industrial Training Board auspices for young people who cannot find an apprenticeship employer. The Boards recruit young people according to an assessment of the future needs of the industry. Toward the end of the initial off-the-job training in ITB centres efforts are made to find employers to continue the apprenticeship. If the ITB is unsuccessful the subsidized training can continue into a second year. The government pays the full cost of training plus £19 a week to the trainee in the first year and £21 in the second year. From July 1975 to July 1977, 11,720 training awards were made.

iv) <u>Construction industry supplementary grants</u>. In order to encourage employers to maintain or increase apprentice intake in an industry which has been exceptionally hard hit by the recession, and to provide a stimulus towards the standard scheme of off-the-job initial training recently introduced by the Construction Industrial Training Board to replace traditional on-the-job training, a grant of up to one-third of the normal CITB grant for approved first year off-the-job training can be made to an employer for an apprentice who is not recruited through a premium grant. From July 1975 to July 1977, 15,200 grants were made.

v) <u>Recruitment grant</u>. An incentive grant not exceeding £1,500 may be paid to an employer who agrees to take on apprentices who began in the Training Award Scheme and cannot find an employer. The employer must complete the apprenticeship training and not reduce his intake of school-leavers as new apprentices.

vi) <u>Continued training</u>. If no employer can be found through the other available schemes the ITB can continue training under its own auspices.

vii) <u>Redundant apprentices' adoption grant.</u> Where an apprentice is laid off at any time up to six months before training is completed and another employer cannot be found under normal arrangements, an incentive grant of £850 in the first two years of apprenticeship and £500 thereafter may be paid to a suitable employer who agrees to complete training and not reduce his intake of new apprentices.

In total 62,000 apprentices who otherwise might not have started an apprenticeship were enabled to undertake training from July 1975 to July 1977. The special subsidies permitted an addition of about 25% to the number of new apprentices.

In Germany special measures to aid unemployed young people also had the effect of enlarging the opportunities for apprenticeship training. Early in 1976 enterprises which had extra training capacity, particularly the railways and the post office, were subsidized to take on young people for a broad-based training which would enable them to obtain employment outside the training enterprise. This was supplemented by a series of other measures designed to secure and expand the supply of apprenticeship and other training places for young people, financed by the federal government and executed in part by the Ministry of Education and in part by the Federal Labour Office. In addition, the Laender had their own programmes for unemployed young people, some of which were directed toward supporting apprenticeship (44).

Several members of the EEC have received grants from the European Social Fund for programmes for unemployed young people. Before mid-1975 the EEC did not give special attention to young people and the Social Fund still may not intervene in the initial training of young people immediately after completion of their term of compulsory schooling. Nevertheless, the availability of EEC monies has encouraged programmes which conform to its terms in several countries.

4. <u>Public Financial Aid to Apprentices</u>

Entrance to apprenticeship usually involves an immediate financial sacrifice since apprentice earnings tend to be lower than those of other young workers. Several governments offer financial inducements to encourage participation in apprenticeship by young people from low income families or from rural or distant areas where extra travel or living costs are involved. West Germany has a scheme called <u>Berufsausbildungsbeihilfe</u>, which is a means-tested allowance for young apprentices whose wages are below a stated amount. The size of the allowance depends on whether the recipients live with their parents or in a special youth hostel. These allowances are paid out of the unemployment insurance fund. In some countries government grants to apprentices to buy tools and equipment are provided either as a right or after a means test. In France salaries paid to apprentices are tax-exempted up to an annual limit of 15,200 F. In Australia one feature of the new CRAFT programme is federal allowances to apprentices who have to live away from home. These allowances are payable during the first and second years of the apprenticeship and are taxable. Several Australian States cover the transportation and living costs of country apprentices and maintain hostels for their accommodation while they are attending technical colleges. Similar provisions exist in Austria, Denmark, Switzerland and other countries. Another form of assistance is to treat apprentices as though they were continuing at school full-time, enabling their parents to receive the children's allowance and claim tax deductions where these are offered. In Ireland, apprentices who are made redundant or become unemployed can receive training allowances from AnCO if they continue their training in the AnCO centres. In some Canadian provinces unemployed apprentices who continue their theoretical education at community colleges can receive government allowances. British programmes to subsidize unemployed apprentices who continue training in centres of industrial training boards follow the same pattern.

In addition to public financial aid in some countries private foundations also make grants or have scholarship programmes for apprentices. In Austria, trade unions offer scholarships to would-be apprentices whose financial situation might prevent them from entering training.

III

CHIEF DEVELOPMENTS IN APPRENTICESHIP IN RECENT YEARS

In a review in 1966 of the apprenticeship systems of eight European countries, seven of which are included in the present survey, it was said that while apprenticeship had been influenced by educational change, social legislation and trends in manpower policies, it had never become a central issue in any one of these three fields. Basic questions of coordination had often remained unsolved (25). In 1977, taking into account the greater diversity of the apprenticeship system of OECD Member countries and the uneven pace and direction of developments and trends, it might be said that significant steps have been taken over the decade to improve apprenticeship. Faced by new imperatives, the countries which regard apprenticeship as an important training method have been modernizing their systems, and the process continues. The aim is not only to correct internal defects and respond to changing technological and economic circumstances, but also to achieve the broader goal of better linking apprenticeship with education on one hand, and with vocational training and employment on the other.

Despite the dangers of generalization, it can be said that the net effect of changes in several countries has been to alter the orientation of apprenticeship so that it now serves the interests of the apprentices and the economy rather more explicitly than in the past. By the same token, the control of employers over the system and their power to direct training to their own needs has been diluted. This effect is more visible in some places than in others and is subject to the ultimate constraint that employers or other sponsors can react by reducing or eliminating apprenticeship places if they feel that changes are too costly, contrary to their interests, or threaten to strip them of authority. The point of resistance is different in each country. A second important phenomenon has been a growing convergence between apprenticeship and vocational education in their respective emphases on general and theoretical education and practical experience.

The background against which these changes in apprenticeship have occurred, which is well-documented in only a few countries and most visible where apprenticeship has been a relatively important system of training, is the declining role of apprenticeship in the modern industry and commerce sector. This is largely due to technological and organisational factors. A preference of some young people for full-time vocational education, and a shift to it for the more theoretical trades, have sapped the strength of apprenticeship in occupations where the two training methods have competed. Moreover, accumulating evidence reveals that the apprenticeship intake of employers during conjunctural downswings runs exactly counter both to the interests of young people who seek apprenticeships more actively at such times and to the longer run needs of the economy for skilled workers.

Nevertheless, in many countries other factors have led to increased interest in expanding and improving apprenticeship. Even where vocational education is clearly the preferred or more prevalent method, attention has been devoted to strengthening apprenticeship. This is partly because of the burden of unemployment among young people and the rising proportions of young people in the labour force until the 1980s. It is also clear that it would be difficult to provide adequate educational facilities for these cohorts in the time available, that to do so might result in unused buildings and classrooms after a few years, and would be very costly. Further, the current interest in modifying classroom education and introducing a work experience element has focussed attention on apprenticeship as a prime example of the combination of work and study. The report of the OECD Joint Working Party on Education and Working Life, and the measures introduced and under consideration in Member countries, point to a renewed interest in utilizing apprenticeship as one of the methods of imparting initial occupational skills. Earlier criticisms of apprenticeship in Germany, although not absent, are muted today and are replaced by efforts to improve practices.

The chief developments in apprenticeship during the past decade may be considered under three headings:

    i)   internal features;

    ii)   the relationship to education; and

    iii) the relationship to other kinds of skill training.

Some countries have experienced few or none of the developments to be detailed and may indeed have rejected them. But these changes are common enough, in different forms, in OECD countries to suggest that certain trends are developing. The extent to which they are implemented or the correspondence between plans and practices is not examined here.

    i)   <u>Internal features</u>

Deliberate attempts are being made through public intervention to increase the number of apprenticeships. Exhortation, legislative changes to ease the situation of employers who offer apprenticeships, financial incentives which provide marginal financing for extra apprentices, payments of some of the costs of all apprentices, or training facilities at little or no cost to the employer, are all being used to increase the total number of apprenticeship posts. The situations that particularly stimulate public action are conjunctural or secular shortfalls in apprentice intake which leave some young people unemployed or which threaten future skills shortages. During the last two or three years several countries have introduced or strengthened measures to subsidize the hiring of apprentices as a major means of helping reduce the unemployment of young people, maintaining training and the future supply of skilled manpower. Several countries have done so by reducing social security charges paid by employers in respect of apprentices. The current German programme, directed toward the absorption of the excess numbers of young people in the age cohorts reaching apprenticeable age up to the early 1980s, is based on the view that the economy will need these extra skilled workers because the demographic trend for the later 1980s will result in inadequate numbers of young people for apprenticeship training. Employers are urged, on the grounds of self-interest, to increase their training intake during the next five years. There are only a few OECD countries where such an appeal might be expected to result in significant action by employers, even with public financing at the margin.

The distribution of apprenticeships is also being influenced by public policy. Attempts are being made through public policy to compensate inadequacies in the availability of apprenticeship places according to geographic location, occupation, type of training situation, sex of the apprentices and other personal and social characteristics. The countries which engage in such activities are not necessarily concerned about every aspect, and in many the public pressure may go no further than a declaration of non-discrimination.

Training is being provided for broader occupational categories by combining apprenticeable occupations. Such an approach to initial training permits an introduction to a broad range of skills and subsequent specialization. The advantages of this training style are that apprentices may defer their decisions to specialize, be more flexible and mobile throughout working life, and can leave the training system with intermediate qualifications and re-enter without penalty. It can also provide a greater uniformity of training and more chances to adapt the pace of learning to individual ability. Several countries are in the process of combining occupations for training and examination purposes. In Germany, for example, it is planned to reduce the present number of 465 training occupations. In the United States, an experimental programme enables apprentices trained in a primary skill in a full programme of 48 months to add a second, related skill after an additional training period of 18 months. Although the reduced number of occupational categories appears to be a contribution to more rational training, some countries are engaged in more basic analyses of employment and of how skills should be grouped for purposes of training. Such efforts affect other forms of vocational education and training as well as apprenticeship.

Training by stages or modules has become the preferred mode of training in an increasing number of occupations and countries. Training by stages is difficult to implement in enterprises, except in the largest ones. It has been closely connected with the development of off-the-premises training centres and has depended on the development of clusters of occupations. Some problems in the practical application of training by stages as well as doubts about its principles have been expressed in countries where legal or formal programmes have been adopted. In 1974 the great majority of German apprenticeship contracts covered only the first stage of training, leaving the apprentices to renegotiate at the end of the period. German and Austrian trade unions are concerned that those who leave training before completing an apprenticeship may not be able to obtain training contracts later, and also that credentials will become devalued and little distinction will remain between those who complete two years and those who complete three years. The German Laender criticized the approach because they would have to adjust the related theoretical training in their schools to correspond to changes in the organisation of the practical training proposed at federal level, and because training by stages covered a group of occupations instead of an occupational sector, which they argued entailed creating several qualification levels within a trade (45). The British Engineering Industrial Training Board, one of the pioneers in changing apprenticeship training methods, recently reviewed the three-stage programme which began with 12-14 weeks of broad-based training. Finding that many trainees became frustrated and resentful because they were delayed in studying the skills of the particular craft they had chosen, they introduced a revised programme that begins with broad-based training in the elementary use of tools, machines and equipment applicable to the chosen craft and leads to a wider range of specializations. In this case, apprentices do not gain an opportunity to change their specialization as they proceed through the stages; it is rarely possible in any case, since employers have hired them for specific crafts. An Australian Apprenticeship Advisory Committee Working Party on industrial training recommended that reviews of trade courses should consider the feasibility of revising them on a modular or similar basis, and that pilot schemes should be considered in selected trades, particularly those with a high practical content. A total strategy for modular training should include teacher development, assessment and design of resource needs, and development of suitable accommodation and equipment (46).

Off-the-job practical training in special centres occupies an increased share of the total training time of apprentices. Two important forms have been developed. The first involves a prolongation of schooling and a special introductory course, as in the Efg in Denmark, the basic vocational training year (Berufsgrundbildungsjahr) in Germany, pre-apprenticeship courses in Australian institutions belonging to the Technical and Further Education sector, and courses in recognized training centres in France. In these programmes young people may not spend any work time at an employer's premises, and in fact may not have an employer during the year. In Germany, however, it may be part of the dual system with time in the enterprise. These programmes have multiple purposes: to maintain a connection with the educational system, to provide a broad instruction to occupations, to make occupational choice easier; to enable the intake of apprentices to be maintained or increased under adverse economic conditions; to correct geographical or other imbalances in the intake, to shorten the duration of apprenticeship training, and to reduce employers' costs. The second form consists of group training centres established for an industry, a group of occupations, a group of firms, or a region. In the first year especially, apprentices tend to spend a continuous period of time in such centres, up to a full year. The existence of such centres promotes the modernization of training syllabuses, greater uniformity of training, wider training for the firms whose own facilities and activities fall short of the required range, opportunities to maintain the intake of trainees either by subsidizing individual employers or by accepting apprenticeship candidates who have no employers, and opportunities to shorten the duration of apprenticeship. The development of this form has not been free of problems, including acceptance by employers, as reports from several countries indicate (47).

The duration of apprenticeship has been reduced and some countries which had a uniform duration for different occupations are tending to establish varying lengths. One of the objectives of shortening apprenticeships is to attract young people who have resisted the longer training because of the consequent delay in achieving full pay as a skilled worker. As education has been prolonged and entrants to apprenticeship are older and have more years of education, the pressures to reduce the time span have mounted, apart from the individual reductions in time for extra education allowed in many countries. Reductions have also been facilitated by other organisational changes that have occurred simultaneously: training by stages, broadened occupational categories and off-the-job training. For employers who have used apprentices in production and have not been able or willing to organise their production so that it would be profitable from the outset, the shortening of the apprenticeship has presented financial problems and stimulated requests for public subsidies. In some quarters, questions have arisen about the trend to reduce the duration, reflecting the fear that it may go too far at the expense of a solid and complete training.

Improvements in the organisation and content of training have been launched. The main elements have been the revision of training syllabuses to take account of changes in industrial and commercial practice and new combinations of occupations; revised examination and certification systems; increased amounts of related schooling, including more general education, often organised as "block" release or "sandwich" courses; better coordination of practical training and theoretical education; increased emphasis on better training and maintenance of standards among training instructors in the firms and centres and teachers in the schools. The German plan for educational development until 1978 calls for a much reduced teacher-pupil ratio in the vocational schools (Berufsschulen) of 1 : 13 and a 50% increase in the minimum time spent at school (from an average of 8.4 hours a week to 12).

The need for new and more equitable forms of financing, both with and without government participation, has gained recognition in several countries. Because employers who train indirectly subsidize those who do not, and because the latter are a majority in most countries, there is a search for forms of financing to spread the costs of all types of training including apprenticeship, to mobilize resources for subsidizing off-the-job training, to regulate variations in the intake of apprentices, and to give incentives to improve training standards within enterprises.

Increased provision has been made for research into training methods, experimentation with model programmes, and other activities by research institutes associated with vocational training. Denmark, Germany, France, the Netherlands, Switzerland and other countries have such activities, and the idea is spreading.

ii) Relationship to education

Efforts have been made to integrate apprenticeship into other forms of education so that it becomes a fully-accredited link between compulsory education and the various forms of secondary and higher education. One signal that a country is treating apprentices as part of the learning force is when the central administrative control of apprenticeship is in the ministry or department of education. The Netherlands did this as early as 1919, Denmark in the post-war period and Germany in 1972. The initial phase of integration takes place in the period before apprenticeship begins. Links between compulsory school and apprenticeship have been forged through the pre-apprenticeship scheme in France which becomes an education-based work-study programme at 14 or 15, legally cutting down the years of compulsory full-time education. The links have also been established by the full year programmes in Germany, Denmark, Australia and by other countries which permit a smooth transition from compulsory education to apprenticeship, encourage the academically less able pupils to enter apprenticeship instead of seeking jobs directly, and provide a buffer for those who cannot find their own apprenticeship places. In the German system it is possible to continue with general education after the basic vocational year.

The second phase of integration occurs during apprenticeship and concerns the general education segment of the apprentice's training. As this is the least developed aspect, only a few experiments can be cited. In response to the apprenticeship reform movement in Germany in the early 1970s, the state of North Rhine-Westphalia reorganised its upper secondary education (Kollegstufe) in order to eliminate the division between general and vocational streams. Apprentices have been permitted to attend regular academic classes together with students preparing for the university and a range of courses suitable to all interests has been designed. Some critics maintain that an essential prerequisite of any attempt to give equality to apprentices in general education is the adoption of comprehensive schools for the compulsory years, so that young people coming from working class backgrounds will be more likely to consider continuing with general education, rather than becoming apprentices.

Perhaps the most important way of incorporating apprenticeship into the educational system has been to treat the completion of apprenticeship as equivalent to the completion of lower or upper secondary education and so as a qualification for entry to the next level of education on a par with academic credentials. A number of northern European countries accept this principle of dual qualification, and it is particularly well developed in Austria. In most of the countries where dual qualifications exist secondary and tertiary education are separated into vocational and academic streams and, in fact, pupils completing an apprenticeship most frequently seek the vocational stream if they continue in full-time education. Some apprenticeships are completed solely for the purposes of gaining entry to a full-time vocational school such as the Fachoberschule in Germany. In the United States some programmes give apprentices the opportunity to work for an associate of arts degree in a two-year community college and to transfer to a four-year academic programme.

iii) Relation to other skill training

The view is spreading that it is outmoded to treat apprenticeship as an independent training system unto itself and it is increasingly regarded as part of a larger system for imparting occupational skills The most convincing evidence that apprenticeship has been integrated into broader training systems is the tendency to abandon the use of the word "apprentice" in preference for "initial or basic vocational training", and to discard "apprenticeable occupations" in favour of "training occupations". Moreover, legislation and governmental programmes have begun to deal with apprenticeship along with other forms of training in a single document or have enacted a series of laws or decrees, reflecting a desire to tie together the various forms of training. In taking this view of apprenticeship, countries are affirming a view expressed in Germany that vocational training is the concern of society as a whole and not only of the employer.

The most successful integration of apprenticeship with overall training has been in arrangements for those who have completed an apprenticeship to obtain technician or higher training in the occupation of their original training. In countries where apprenticeship is the predominant method of acquiring skill training in a large variety of occupations, facilities and opportunities for adult training or retraining are also well worked out and undisputed. Such systems are also well accepted in France and Belgium where vocational education is the primary method of initial skill training. Apprenticeship and alternative full-time vocational education have not been well integrated in most countries, especially where they serve as competing methods for the same occupations, as in France and Austria. The most troubling aspect of this has been the resistance in certain of the English-speaking countries to the extension of apprenticeship to adults and the acceptance of alternative training methods for them. This issue is closely related to the role of the trade unions in apprenticeship regulation and administration.

IV

ISSUES AND POLICY IMPLICATIONS

The developments outlined in the previous section have certainly not penetrated into every country, nor are they spread evenly in all apprenticeship fields within the countries where these ideas have been introduced. Moreover, the practical difficulties of implementing the newer initiatives and coordinating them with the existing body of apprenticeship operations still have to be worked out. Further, it must be recognized that to adopt the principle that apprenticeship constitutes a qualification for entrance to additional general education and to provide the appropriate educational mechanisms will not necessarily ensure that the pupils who complete apprenticeships will in fact pursue higher education to the same degree as others who follow more traditional educational paths. Nor does the legislative establishment of schemes to offer adults opportunities to enter apprenticeship or to gain equivalent skill training necessarily yield the numbers of skilled workers required by the economy, if obstacles to their acceptance cannot be overcome. It is, therefore, not surprising that the improvement and extension of apprenticeship along lines identified in Part III have not overcome all the objections to apprenticeship which have accumulated over the years.

Some of the issues in apprenticeship are inherent and apply to all countries, but others are specific to individual countries or groups of countries. Some problems are long-standing while others arise out of the more recent improvements and developments. Many if not all of the issues in apprenticeship reflect the tensions between employers' desire for a skill training method to meet their needs and other pressures from individuals, workers' representatives and other interests, to treat apprenticeship as a training system which imparts broad, transferable skills and is part of the range of educational opportunities, providing access to other types and levels of education.

Criticisms of Apprenticeship

While the many advantages of apprenticeship are recognized several important criticisms have been made. They are considered in turn (48).

Too many apprentices, especially in small- and medium-sized firms, are primarily part of the productive process and receive training only when it fits the production schedule. The general and related education they receive is inadequate and poorly coordinated with practical training. It cannot be said with accuracy how many apprentices in individual countries are in this situation or whether the position is inherent to the operations of these enterprises. To the extent that remedies can be applied, they lie in the implementation and enforcement of the types of measures described in Part III. Earlier opposition to below-par apprenticeship as "cheap labour" has been somewhat muted by findings, such as those of the Edding Commission in Germany, that the majority of enterprises incur positive training costs for apprenticeship, even when the quality of the training leaves much to be desired (16). Interviews with representatives of smaller enterprises, especially in the craft sector, reveal that the current emphasis on calculating the costs of training may discourage some employers from offering apprenticeships, since they have previously not calculated their costs and may have believed that no net costs were involved. There may at present be greater tolerance of below-par training in countries where the numbers of young people are growing and an expansion of apprenticeship places is sought. On-the-job experience is considered a good thing in itself as a transition measure, and even superior to school training for some young people, and an expansion of the number of school places is time-consuming and costly. For these reasons there is a trade-off between imposing strict apprenticeship standards which discourage training and accepting inadequacy in some quarters while slowly trying to improve conditions.

Co-operation among small enterprises to establish group training centres demands a high degree of commitment to training and its organisation which often exceed the possibilities for initiative by individual firms. While this view is true, it ignores the power of government leadership and financial assistance to overcome the weakness of individual enterprises and help initiate collaborative arrangements, as has occurred in Germany, the United Kingdom and France, among others.

The quality and quantity of the instructors in enterprises, training centres and schools which offer related and general education are often below the necessary standards of competence. Schools and training centres are sometimes poorly equipped with teaching materials and machinery. Since these complaints are equally valid for many institutions of full-time vocational education and other training methods, they are not inherent defects of apprenticeship and are remediable.

Apprenticeship may lead to a narrow specialization and inadequate occupational flexibility and mobility. This point was well put by the task force which reviewed training in Ontario, Canada. Commenting on the fact that in Ontario the apprenticeship system recognized only full training as an all-round journeyman and offered no credits for a completed apprenticeship to someone who wished to learn another trade, the report states:

> "we doubt the continuing viability of a training system that recognizes only one level of competence and discourages mobility between trade areas" [20].

The situation is somewhat better in countries which have developed training by stages and offer credit for a prior apprenticeship, but the major difference in Germany, Austria and Switzerland is in the easy mobility among occupations. The completion of an apprenticeship in itself is a credential, widely accepted by an employer as evidence of good work habits and an ability to learn. Under the favourable conditions of full and overfull employment and the absence of craft union restrictions, few complaints arose about restrictions on occupational mobility. Rather the question arose as to whether training was not too specific and too divided into separate occupations to permit the substitutability of one kind of apprenticeship for another. Thus the narrowness argument is generally accepted; but the experience with inadequate mobility is not universal and perhaps must be tested in a prolonged less-than-full employment situation in northern Europe. In any case, narrow training and undue specialization is also possible in full-time vocational education, as in France, where the CAP diploma can be earned in several hundred occupational specialities. Where vocational education offers clusters of skills rather than particular occupations, the training may be considered too general by employers and may need to be supplemented. The training-by-stages approach in apprenticeship and the integration of apprenticeship with other training systems can help avoid too narrow specialization. Nevertheless, a certain tension always remains in apprenticeship between the employer's desire for specific training and the trainee's need for a broader base which also better meets the requirements of the economy.

The number and kind of openings for vocational training in private enterprises are dependent on regional economic structure and on general economic development. This is an acknowledged weakness of apprenticeship; the number of openings responds to conjunctural forces and regional differences in industrial structure rather than the number and occupational desires of the potential trainees. It is not an equal weakness of vocational education, although it is also differentiated regionally and reflects the types of jobs available locally. Some time will be required to discover whether the various programmes to smooth out conjunctural variations in apprentice intake result in unemployed apprentices after the first off-the-job year of training. In a prolonged period of high unemployment employers may not absorb the output of the training centres, and an alternative training method may be needed. In countries where apprenticeship is the predominant method regional deficiencies in the number and variety of apprenticeship openings can probably best be remedied by supplementing apprenticeship with vocational education.

All efforts to reform the apprenticeship system have found it extremely difficult to solve the questions of financing and costs sharing. Undoubtedly, the rise in training costs experienced by employers has induced some of them to consider whether they can continue training apprentices, especially in enterprises in which long-run technological and organisational changes have suggested a declining need for apprentices in certain job categories. The pressure on governments to devise collective financing measures such as already exist in several countries is considerable, because when the cost of apprenticeship is borne by an employer or groups of employers there is a saving of the public expenditure that otherwise would have been needed to provide more places in full-time educational institutions.

Other Issues

The spread of off-the-job practical training centres has created coordination problems with the older type of release from the firm for related theoretical and general education. Each of the parties involved, enterprises, apprentices, training centres and schools, report that the spread of the work-week or year among three institutions presents difficulties. Enterprises, facing an erratically diminished labour supply and a loss of work time when apprentices have to travel, become eager to use almost all time in the firm for direct production. Apprentices feel confused by the different sources of instruction. There is overlap at times between the training centres and the schools in subject matters; and programmes of work, training and education are not always coordinated. The newer training centres in several countries claim that they could offer the theoretical and general education as well as the established educational institutions: the latter naturally disagree and feel threatened. In France, where there has never been great satisfaction with the part-time education system for apprentices, there has been a move to solve this problem by giving the new centres for apprenticeship training (CFA) responsibility for the practical, theoretical and general aspects. In Australia Technical and Further Education (TAFE) institutions have combined the practical training and theoretical education, and could add the general education if that should ever become a required part of apprenticeship.

The practical experience component in vocational education and the development of other training methods has made them competitive with apprenticeship for places with employers. This problem arises mostly in countries which have a high proportion of the age-group in apprenticeship and an area of overlap between apprenticeship and vocational education. In Germany there are the beginnings of such competition, with the Praktikant somewhat favoured because of a shorter period in the firm. In France there is no practical component in vocational education which leads to the CAP or BEP examinations. As other countries introduce programmes combining work and study on a large scale they may find that employers choose one type of training rather than another, but in the English-speaking countries the restricted fields for apprenticeship may protect this form of training.

The improvement of working conditions for young workers may be discouraging to employers. Legislation or collective agreements to reduce the working day or week can deprive employers of apprentices at the time they are often most needed and increase the rising costs of apprenticeship. Whilst governments can to some extent help reduce such costs they may find it more difficult to reconcile the needs of enterprises with the protection of young people at work.

The rapid growth of vocational education, often as a substitute for or rival of apprenticeship, has led to comparisons to the detriment of apprenticeship. Criticisms of apprenticeship have led some commentators to conclude that vocational education is preferable. However a blanked endorsement of vocational education, without specific reference to types and levels of occupations, ignores the differences in the suitability of the two methods to the characteristics of an occupation. Furthermore, account has to be taken of the differences among countries in commitment to each form of training: in the long run apprenticeship may remain viable in one country, but not in another. Finally, all judgements about the efficacy of either method are made in the absence of hard research material on the actual outcomes of each method applied to comparable training groups. Since a preference for vocational education is not based solely on the criterion of occupational skill training, the balance must also take into account its other functions. Evaluation of the various alternative ways of organising vocational education and training for young people requires more attention.

It may be difficult to expand the number of places for apprentices. In countries where a limited range of occupations is apprenticeable, the use of a variety of financial incentives has had limited success; and it may not be possible to expand the intake into apprenticeship, short of full government financing of net training costs. Thus far, the German government has had some success in this direction through an appeal to employers and the threat of a tax. However, the main response in Germany has been from the artisan sector, and it is disputed whether these are the occupations in which training is most needed by individuals and the economy. Although there is general agreement that apprenticeship in any field serves well to socialize young people into the world of work, for some it may merely postpone the occupational choices and job search which would otherwise occur at the end of schooling.

Since the essence of apprenticeship is the establishment of an employment relationship, the numbers and types of training places available are limited. One limitation is the willingness and ability of employers to train within a formal apprenticeship system. Another is the level of employment. Current and prospective high levels of unemployment and, in particular, the fall to a very low level of new jobs for young people also restricts their access to enterprise training including apprenticeship and imposes a serious limitation on the future supply of skilled manpower. Consideration of the training of young people and their transition to working life must therefore proceed beyond a consideration of apprenticeship in the context of other forms of training, including other forms of training by employers and education-based systems which combine study and work, especially since the latter are growing at a more rapid rate than either apprenticeship or employer programmes in almost every country.

REFERENCES

1. Education and Working Life in Modern Society, OECD, Paris, 1975, p. 24.

2. Bildungswesen im Vergleich. No. 5, Darstellung des beruflichen Bildungswesens in ausgewählten Ländern, WEMA-Institut. Koblenz, 1974;
Mission to Study Methods of Training Skilled Workers in Europe. The Training of Skilled Workers in Europe. Melbourne, 1970;
European Apprenticeship. CIRF Monographs, Vol. 1, No. 2, International Labour Office, Geneva, Switzerland, 1966;
G. Williams. Apprenticeship in Europe. Chapman and Hall, London, 1963.

3. Apprenticeship: A New Approach, AnCO, The Industrial Training Authority. Dublin, 1973.

4. The New Apprenticeship: Decisions of Council of AnCO, AnCO. The Industrial Training Authority. Dublin, October 1975.

5. Betriebliche Berufsausbildung, Institut für angewandte Sozialwissenschaft. Bonn, December 1974;
Bildung und Wissenschaft. No. 9, 1977, p. 145;
Social Report. No. 4, 1977, pp. 1-3.

6. Ørum. Fra skole til erhverv. The Danish National Institute of Social Research. Meddelelse No. 7. Copenhagen, 1974.

7. M. Croisier. La scolarité des apprentis vaudois (incidences pour l'orientation professionnelle). Service de la formation professionnelle. Lausanne, 1971;
Die Situation am Lehrstellenmarkt. Institut für angewandte Sozialwissenschaft. Bonn, August 1975.

8. Apprenticeship Statistics 1966-1976. Australian Apprenticeship Advisory Committee, Melbourne.

9. The Craftsman in Engineering. Engineering Industrial Training Board. Watford, 1975.

10. J. P. Mitchell. "New Directions for Apprenticeship Policy". Worklife, US Department of Labor, Employment and Training Administration, January 1977.

11. R. W. Glover. "Apprenticeship in America: An Assessment". Proceedings, Industrial Relations Research Association. December 1974.

12. E. G. Green. "Apprenticeship: A Potential Weapon Against Minority Youth Unemployment", in National Commission for Manpower Policy. From School to Work. Washington; G. P. O., 1976;
Glover, op. cit.;
See also F. R. Marshall and V. M. Briggs, Jr. Equal Apprenticeship Opportunities: The Nature of the Issue and the New York Experience. The Institute of Labor and Industrial Relations, University of Michigan-Wayne State University, Ann Arbor, and the National Manpower Policy Task Force, 1968.

13. Internationes Press Service. Social Report. No. 10, 1976, pp. 4-5;
Ibid; Sonderdienst. No. 15, 1973.

14. Berufsbildung 1975/76. DIHT (Deutscher Industrie - und Handelstag). Bonn, 1976.

15. L'Apprentissage. ONISEP. Paris, January 1975.

16. Sachverständigenkommission Kosten und Finanzierung der beruflichen Bildung. Kosten und Finanzierung der ausserschulischen beruflichen Bildung. (Edding Commission); Abschlussbericht. Bertelsmann, Bielefeld, 1974;
F. Stooss. "Zur regionalen Ungleichheit der beruflichen Bildungschancen der Bundesrepublik Deutschland". Mitteilungen aus der Arbeitsmarkt- und Berufsforschung. No. 2, 1971;
U. Schwarz and F. Stooss, "Zur regionalen Ungleichheit der beruflichen Bildungschancen und Vorschläge zum Abbau des Gefälles" Mitteilungen aus der Arbeitsmarkt- und Berufsforschung. No. 2, 1973.

17. H. Hofbauer and H. Kraft. "Betriebliche Berufsausbildung und Erwerbstätigkeit. Betriebs- und Berufswechsel bei männlichen Erwerbspersonen nach Abschluss der betrieblichen Berufsausbildung". Mitteilungen aus der Arbeitsmarkt- und Berufsforschung. No. 1, 1974;
I. Speiser. Mobilität junger Berufstätiger. Österreichisches Institut Bildung and Wissenschaft. Vienna, 1976, 2 vols.;
R. Weiss. Die Berufsausbildung und Berufslaufbahn von Lehrlingen. Arbeiterkammern für Tirol und Salzburg, 1974;
Department of Employment Gazette (Great Britain), July 1975, pp. 623-626;

Enquête sur le devenir des jeunes issus de l'apprentissage artisanal en 1970. Assemblée permanente des chambres de métiers, Paris, October 1976;
A. Goldschmidt. L'évolution professionnelle des anciens apprentis. Office d'orientation et de formation professionnelle du Département du commerce, de l'industrie et du travail. Geneva, 1972;
J. Rousselet et al. "L'entrée des jeunes dans la vie active". Cahiers du centre d'études de l'emploi. No. 7, 1975 and follow-up in a forthcoming issue.

18. Ausbildung der Ausbilder. Ministry of Education and Science. Bonn, 1976.

19. Member State Report by the Federal Republic of Germany, annex to the report by the Education Committee of the European Communities on the "Preparation for Working Life and for Transition from Education to Work". Ministry of Education and Science. Bonn, August 1976.

20. Training for Ontario's Future. Ministry of Colleges and Universities. Toronto, 1973.

21. Note sur l'apprentissage. Ministère de l'Education, Direction des Lycées, Division de l'apprentissage. Paris, 12th May, 1976.

22. Berufsbildung 1975/76. Deutscher Industrie- und Handelstag (DIHT). Bonn, 1976, Table 3;
Berufliche Aus- und Fortbildung 1975. Ministry of Education and Science, Bonn, 1976.

23. Lehrlingsstatistik 1975. Bundeskammer der gewerblichen Wirtschaft.

24. H. Hofbauer and F. Stooss. "Defizite und Überschüsse an betrieblichen Ausbildungsplätzen nach Wirtschafts- und Berufsgruppen". Mitteilungen aus der Arbeitsmarkt- und Berufsforschung. No. 2, 1976.

25. Green, op. cit.

26. Ansprache des Bundeskanzlers auf der Meisterfeier der Handwerkskammer Düsseldorf. Presse- und Informationsamt der Bundesregierung. Bulletin, 17th March 1977, p. 239.

27. H. Hofbauer and F. Stooss, op. cit.;
B. G. Reubens. "German Apprenticeship: Controversy and Reform". Manpower. November 1973.

28. Employment and Productivity Gazette. 1969-1977.

29. Skilled Engineering Shortages in a High-Demand Area. Department of Employment. Manpower Papers No. 3, 1971; The Craftsman in Engineering. Engineering Industry Training Board, Watford, 1975.

30. European Apprenticeship. CIRF Monographs, Vol. 1, No. 2, International Labour Office, Geneva, 1966.

31. H. von Henninges and U. Schwarz. "Zur Ausbildungsintensität von Industriebetrieben". Mitteilungen aus der Arbeitsmarkt- und Berufsforschung. No. 2, 1975; H. von Henninges. "Bestimmungsgründe des Umfangs der Facharbeiternachwuchsausbildung in der Industrie". Mitteilungen aus der Arbeitsmarkt- und Berufsforschung. No. 4, 1975.

32. Among the published studies are:
N. Woodward. "Costing the Tradesman's Entrance", Personnel Management. November 1975;
N. Woodward and T. Anderson. "A Profitability Appraisal of Apprenticeships". British Journal of Industrial Relations. July 1975;
N. Woodward. "Break-even Points and Off-the-job Training". European Training. Vol. 2, No. 3;
BACIE. A Standard Method of Costing the Training of Apprentices. BACIE Journal. September 1963;
B. Thomas, J. Moxham and J. A. G. Jones. "A Cost-Benefit Analysis of Industrial Training". British Journal of Industrial Relations. July 1969;
M. Oatey. "The Economics of Training with Respect to the Firm". British Journal of Industrial Relations. March 1970;
S. Mukherjee. Changing Manpower Needs. PEP, London, 1970;
"Cost of First-Year Training for Engineering Craftsmen and Technicians". UK Engineering Industry Training Board. Research, Planning and Statistics Division. Working Paper No. 2/75. Watford, April 1976;
M. Woodhall. "Investment in Industrial Training: An Assessment of the Effects of the Industrial Training Act on the Volume and Costs of Training". British Journal of Industrial Relations. March 1974;
H. Wahrmut. Die Kosten und Erträge der Lehrlingshaltung im Handwerk. Bund-Verlag G. m. b. H., Köln-Deutz, 1957;
Warth. Lehrlingausbildung und Ausbildungskosten (Handwerk, Industrie). Forschungsberichte aus dem Handwerk. Handwerkswissenschaftliches Institut, Münster-Westfalen, 1963, vol. 8;
Wernet. Über die Lehrlingshaltung im Handwerk in wirtschaftlicher Sicht. Handwerkswissenschaftliches Institut, Münster-Westfalen, 1958, vol. 2.

33. The Edding Commission. op. cit. See also, other German studies discussed in the Edding Commission Report.

34. M. Zymelman. The Economic Evaluation of Vocational Training Programs. World Bank Staff Occasional Papers No. 21. John Hopkins Press, Baltimore, 1976;
N. Woodward. "The Feasibility of Evaluating Apprentice Training". European Training. Vol. 3, No. 3;
N. Woodward. "The Economic Evaluation of Apprentice Training". Industrial Relations Journal. Spring 1975.

35. Training Services Agency. Manpower Services Commission. Report of Working Party on Collective Funding. November 1976.

36. For a detailed history of the evolution and passage of the 1964 Act, see P. J. C. Perry. The Evolution of British Manpower Policy, London, 1976;
B. O. Pettman. "Industrial Training in Great Britain". International Journal of Social Economics. Vol. 1, No. 1, 1974.

37. Engineering Employers' Federation. Manpower in Engineering. Report by an EEF Study Group. London, April 1976.

38. Department of Employment and Manpower Services Commission. Training for Vital Skills: A consultative document. London, 1976, p. 11. For other evaluations see:
M. Woodhall. op. cit. ;
B. O. Pettman. Ed. , Training and Retraining: A Basis for the Future. Transcripta, London, 1973;
B. O. Pettman. The Industrial Training Act and the Work of the Industrial Training Boards: A Selected and Annotated Bibliography. Institute of Scientific Business, Bradford, 1973.

39. B. O. Pettman. "Industrial Training - who pays ?", Education and Training. October 1974.

40. Training for Skills: A programme for action. Manpower Services Commission. London, 1977.

41. Worklife, US Department of Labor, Employment and Training Administration, August 1977.

42. Apprenticeship: The Nucleus of Craftsmanship. 1976 Report of the Administrator, Bureau of Apprenticeship and Training. US Department of Labour, Washington, 1976.

43. Young People at Work. Manpower Services Commission. London, May 1977, App. 2.

44. From Education to Working Life. Bulletin of the European Communities, Supplement 12/76, Luxembourg, 1976.

45. W. Maslankowski. "Stufenausbildung - Stand der Einführung und Auswirkungen". Die berufsbildende Schule. September 1975;
Analyse der Probleme mit der Stufenausbildung. Industriegewerkschaft Metall, Frankfurt, July 1976;
Education in Germany. Internationes. No. 3, 1971.

46. Observations on Modular Training. Australian Apprenticeship Advisory Committee. Melbourne, November 1975.

47. Zum Problem zwischenbetrieblicher Ausbildungsmassnahmen in Österreich. Österreichisches Institut für Bildung und Wirtschaft. Vienna, 1976;
B. Delventhal and G. Holzel. "Die übertriebliche Ausbildung im Handwerk". Die Deutsche Berufs- und Fachschule. April 1976;
G. Marwitz. "Realisierungsprobleme der Berufsbildungsreform, dargestellt am Beispiel der Berufsgrundbildungsjahr-Anrechnungsverordnung". Berufsbildung in Wissenschaft und Praxis. August 1975.

48. From Education to Working Life. Bulletin of the European Communities, Supplement 12/76. Luxembourg, 1976.

Appendix

STATISTICAL TABLES

Table 1. NEW APPRENTICES IN SELECTED OECD COUNTRIES, 1950 TO 1975

Thousands

YEAR	AUSTRALIA	AUSTRIA	GERMANY a)	SWITZER-LAND	UNITED STATES
	1	2	3	4	5
1950	..	..	291	27	60
1951	..	..	303	28	64
1952	..	..	318	28	63
1953	..	..	344	28	74
1954	..	..	403	28	59
1955	..	..	415	30	67
1956	..	..	406	31	74
1957	..	..	377	33	60
1958	..	..	384	35	50
1959	..	..	364	37	66
1960	..	..	336	41	54
1961	..	..	367	43	49
1962	..	..	..	44	56
1963	..	50	482	46	57
1964	..	48	484	46	60
1965	..	47	487	45	68
1966	28	15 b)	461	45	85
1967	28	42	490	44	98
1968	28	45	463	44	111
1969	32	44	398	45	123
1970	35	45	452	45	107
1971	33	50	457	47	78
1972	32	50	460	48	104
1973	42	53	458	50	133
1974	36	55	430	52	113
1975	36	56	..	53	83

NOTES:
a) Excluding agriculture and including Anlernlinge, 1950-1961. Including Praktikanten, 1963-1974.
b) Due to change in the school-leaving age.

SOURCES: National data on new contracts, new registrations or first year apprentices.

Table 2. ACTIVITIES OF YOUNG PEOPLE, GERMANY, 1960 TO 1974: PROPORTION OF YOUNG PEOPLE AGED 15-18 IN EACH ACTIVITY

YEAR	APPRENTICE-SHIP[a] (%)	OTHER WORK OR UNEMPLOYED (%)	FULL-TIME VOCATIONAL EDUCATION (%)	GYMNASIUM (%)	OTHER GENERAL EDUCATION (%)	TOTAL NUMBER AGED 15-18 (000,000)
	1	2	3	4	5	6
1960	46.7	10.7	9.2	7.3	26.1	..
1961	47.6	10.5	9.6	7.4	25.9	..
1962	48.7	10.5	9.8	7.0	24.0	2.7
1963	51.2	11.2	10.1	6.6	20.9	2.7
1964	48.4	10.4	9.8	6.0	25.4	3.0
1965	47.3	10.1	10.0	6.4	26.2	3.1
1966	46.1	9.1	10.3	7.1	27.4	3.2
1967	47.5	8.6	11.3	8.6	24.0	3.2
1968	47.4	8.0	11.8	9.0	23.8	3.2
1969	44.0	7.1	12.6	9.3	27.0	3.2
1970	43.0	6.8	13.3	9.9	27.0	..
1971	41.7	6.2	14.9	10.1	27.1	3.3
1972	41.4	5.8	16.4	10.4	26.0	3.4
1973	42.6	5.8	17.0	11.4	23.2	3.5
1974	41.5	5.3	17.0	11.7	24.5	3.6

NOTES: a) Includes Anlernlinge.
.. Not available.
SOURCE: Federal Republic of Germany, BMBW, Berufsbildung, Ausbildungsplatzangebot fur Jugendliche in Betrieb und Schule, Bonn, September 1974, Table 2. Statistisches Jahrbuch fur die Bundesrepublik Deutschland. Stuttgart: Kohlhammer, annual.

Table 3. ACTIVITIES OF YOUNG PEOPLE AFTER COMPULSORY SCHOOL, AUSTRIA, 1957, 1960 AND 1970/71 TO 1975/76: PROPORTION OF SCHOOL-LEAVERS IN EACH ACTIVITY

YEAR	APPRENTICESHIP (%)	OTHER WORK OR UNEMPLOYMENT (%)	FULL-TIME VOCATIONAL EDUCATION (%)	ACADEMIC EDUCATION (%)	TOTAL SCHOOL-LEAVERS (000)
	1	2	3	4	5
1957	33.0	40.0	17.5	9.5	
1960	40.0	30.5	18.0	11.5	
1970/71	51.0	16.3	18.7	14.0	105
1971/72	50.4	14.8	19.7	15.2	110
1972/73	50.8	12.3	22.2	15.6	113
1973/74	51.9	10.4	22.4	15.2	115
1974/75	52.4	9.5	23.4	14.7	118
1975/76	53.5	7.4	24.3	14.8	122

SOURCES: 1957, 1960, ILO, CIRF Monographs, European Apprenticeship, Geneva, 1966, p. 206; 1970/71 to 1975/76, Österreichischer Gewerkschaftsbund and Österreichischer Arbeitskammertag, Jugend am Arbeitsmarkt, Vienna, 1976, Table 3, p. 8.

Table 4. APPRENTICESHIP OF YOUNG PEOPLE AFTER COMPULSORY SCHOOL, SWITZERLAND, 1965 TO 1975

Proportion of school-leavers in apprenticeship

YEAR	APPRENTICESHIP %	TOTAL SCHOOL-LEAVERS (100)
	1	2
1965	45.8	98.1
1966	46.5	96.8
1967	47.6	93.1
1968	47.8	92.8
1969	50.3	88.9
1970	52.2	87.4
1971	53.3	88.4
1972	53.7	90.4
1973	53.8	92.5
1974	55.6	92.7
1975	56.1	94.1

SOURCE: National authorities.

Table 5. RATIOS OF APPRENTICES TO SKILLED WORKERS IN SELECTED COUNTRIES

COUNTRY	OCCUPATION	RATIO APPRENTICES : SKILLED WORKERS NORMAL	CAN THE NORMAL RATIO BE EXCEEDED
	1	2	3
Australia	a)	1 : 3	Yes
Austria	Artisan crafts	3 : 1	If a master craftsman qualified in more than one occupation
	Industry	3 : 2 to 51 : 50 Over 51, 3 to 5 skilled persons to each apprentice	If a full-time qualified instructor present
Ireland	a)	1 : 3	Yes
New Zealand	Engineering	1 : 1	Yes
Switzerland	Auto-mechanic " "	1 : 1 to 4 : 4 Then 4 skilled workers for each additional apprentice	Yes
	Commerce "	1 : 1 to 3 : 5-8 Then 1-4 additional skilled workers for each apprentice	Second apprentice may begin in last year of other apprentice

a) Most or all for apprenticeable occupations.

SOURCE: National legislation, regulations and negotiated agreements.

Table 6. PERCENTAGE OF APPRENTICES TO SKILLED WORKERS[a]
ALBERTA, CANADA, 1970 TO 1975

TRADE	1970	1971	1972	1973	1974	1975
	1	2	3	4	5	6
Carpenters	26.7	23.8	19.8	25.4	19.8	29.5
Electricians	70.0	64.6	56.5	62.6	56.5	60.6
Plumbers	64.6	57.6	55.8	54.7	55.9	59.4
Steamfitters	49.3	40.5	31.5	24.5	31.7	18.9
Gasfitters	18.9	17.1	20.0	19.5	20.0	14.8
Welders	26.3	23.4	27.9	33.0	28.0	42.9
Sheet Metal Workers	57.7	55.3	49.2	43.9	49.4	46.5
Heavy Duty Mechanics	44.3	42.9	41.2	51.3	41.4	69.7
Ironworkers	33.0	9.4	33.6	10.3	25.4	19.5
Millwrights	33.7	30.5	24.3	21.4	25.2	30.7
Insulators	n.a.	n.a.	20.9	55.4	19.8	31.1
Bricklayers	12.8	10.8	12.9	21.4	24.7	28.1
Machinists	31.1	21.1	17.1	22.7	23.2	22.8
Motor Mechanics	28.3	27.4	28.0	31.2	34.7	35.0
Decorator-Painters	12.5	16.5	12.7	14.2	17.8	11.0

NOTE: a) Calculated from actual employment.

SOURCE: Shop inspection surveys.

Table 7. ACTIVE JOURNEYMEN PER APPRENTICE, UNITED STATES, 1962

TRADE	ACTIVE JOURNEYMEN PER APPRENTICE[a]
1	2
Bricklayers[b]	20
Carpenters	21
Electricians	9
Ironworkers	23
Painters, paperhangers and glaziers	26
Plasterers and cement masons	20
Plumbers and pipefitters	10
Roofers[c]	8
Sheet metal workers	8
Pressmen, book and job	9
Pressmen, news	9
Stereo and electrotyper, book and job	14
Stereo and electrotyper, news	12
Typographer, book and job	10
Typographer, news	17
Photoengraver, book and job	11
Photoengraver, news	12
Bookbinders, book and job	11
Mailers, book and job	42
Mailers, news	28

NOTES: a) The ratio of the number of journeymen working or available for work, to the number of persons working under apprenticeship agreements.
b) Includes marble setter, mosaic terrazzo layer, stonemason, and tile setter.
c) Roofer: composition, slate, and tile.

SOURCE: National authorities

Table 8. RATIOS OF APPRENTICES TO SKILLED WORKERS: VICTORIA, AUSTRALIA, 1974-75 ACTUAL RATIOS AND RATIOS REQUIRED TO MEET ESTIMATED NEED FOR SKILLED WORKERS

TRADE	APPRENTICES NUMBERS	ESTIMATED SKILLED WORK FORCE	RATIO APPRENTICES : SKILLED WORKERS ACTUAL	ESTIMATED RATIO REQUIRED
Building:				
Carpentry and joinery	4,104	20,000	1 : 5	1 : 4
Plumbing	2,231	10,000	1 : 4.5	1 : 5
Bricklaying	755	5,000	1 : 6.5	1 : 4
Electrical:				
Mechanics, fitters, etc.	3,600	16,000	1 : 4.5	1 : 4
Radio	411	3,000	1 : 7.5	1 : 5
Metal:				
Engineering	4,033	35,000	1 : 8.7	1 : 5
Boilermaking	1,158	10,000	1 : 8.6	1 : 5
Sheet metal	546	4,300	1 : 8	1 : 5
Automotive:				
Motor mechanics	4,679	20,000	1 : 4.3	1 : 4
Vehicle	1,365	4,500	1 : 3.3	1 : 3
Printing	1,299	6,600	1 : 5	1 : 5

SOURCE: Apprenticeship Commission of Victoria, Annual Report 1975, p. 10.

Table 9. MANPOWER IN ENGINEERING[a], GREAT BRITAIN, 1965, 1968, 1970 AND 1972 TO 1974, DISTRIBUTION BY TYPE OF WORK

Percentages

TYPE OF WORK	1965	1968	1970	1972	1973	1974
	1	2	3	4	5	6
Managerial	3.2	3.4	3.5	3.8	3.9	4.0
Scientists and technologists	1.7	1.9	1.9	1.8	1.8	1.8
Technicians (incl. draughtsmen)	6.2	7.3	7.4	7.6	7.5	7.3
Admin. and professional	} 15.8	3.7	4.1	4.3	4.4	4.4
Clerical and office		12.6	12.3	12.1	11.6	11.5
Supervisors (incl. foremen)	3.1	4.1	4.2	4.6	4.6	4.7
Craftsmen	29.9	20.9	19.7	19.9	19.4	18.7
Operators	23.9	32.1	34.3	33.3	34.1	35.2
All others (excl. canteen)	14.0	14.0	12.6	12.6	12.7	12.4
Total	100.0	100.0	100.0	100.0	100.0	100.0

NOTE: a) Excluding foundries.

SOURCE: Engineering Industry Training Board.

Table 10. MANPOWER IN THE FOUNDRY INDUSTRY, GREAT BRITAIN, 1968, 1970 AND 1972 TO 1974 DISTRIBUTION BY TYPE OF WORK

Percentages

CATEGORY	1968	1970	1972	1973	1974
Managers and supervisors	7.8	8.2	9.1	9.0	8.9
Technologists and technicians	2.6	2.5	2.7	2.5	2.4
Admin. and clerks	8.7	8.7	8.6	8.4	8.5
Craftsmen	20.4	18.7	19.5	17.9	17.4
Operators	47.6	49.1	50.8	52.4	52.9
Other occupations	12.2	11.9	9.2	9.8	9.9
Unspecified	0.7	0.9	0.1	–	–
Total	100.0	100.0	100.0	100.0	100.0

SOURCE: Engineering Industry Training Board, Annual Reports and Accounts.

Table 11. CRAFT APPRENTICES AND SKILLED WORKERS, ENGINEERING[a]
GREAT BRITAIN, 1964 TO 1974

YEAR	APPRENTICES '000	SKILLED WORKERS '000	APPRENTICES: SKILLED WORKERS[d] RATIO
	1	2	3

Engineering and related industries[b]

1964	130	830	1 : 6.4
1965	133	838	1 : 6.3
1966[e]	133	856	1 : 6.5
1967	131	798	1 : 6.1
1968	128	794	1 : 6.2
1969	121	777	1 : 6.4
1970[f]	112	802	1 : 7.1
1971	109	788	1 : 7.2
1972	95	754	1 : 7.9
1973[g]	80	692	1 : 8.6
1974	72	688	1 : 9.5

Shipbuilding and ship repairing[c]

1964	10	50	1 : 4.9
1965	10	54	1 : 5.4
1966[e]	10	56	1 : 5.7
1967	10	57	1 : 5.6
1968	10	58	1 : 5.7
1969	9	56	1 : 6.0
1970[f]	9	57	1 : 6.4
1971	8	57	1 : 7.1
1972	9	57	1 : 6.1
1973[g]	9	53	1 : 6.1
1974	8	52	1 : 6.8

Total

1964	140	880	1 : 6.3
1965	143	893	1 : 6.2
1966[e]	142	912	1 : 6.4
1967	141	854	1 : 6.1
1968	139	852	1 : 6.1
1969	130	834	1 : 6.4
1970[f]	121	859	1 : 7.1
1971	117	845	1 : 7.2
1972	105	810	1 : 7.7
1973[g]	89	745	1 : 8.4
1974	80	740	1 : 9.3

NOTES:
a) In enterprises employing 11 or more workers in May each year.
b) Except shipbuilding.
c) Figures for shipbuilding and shiprepairing are less complete than for engineering generally, but the greater part of the industry is covered.
d) Ratios vary between the different sectors within industries.
e) Skilled men includes non-apprentice trainees who for technical reasons could not be separately identified from the 1966 survey results. In the remaining years the number of non-apprentice male trainees for skilled occupations ranged (in total) between 13,000 in 1974 and 24,350 in 1967.
f) Change of Standard Industrial Classification (SIC) 1958 to SIC 1968 from June 1969, effective from the 1970 enquiry.
g) After 1972 the basis for grossing up the sample was changed from estimates derived from National Insurance Card counts to estimates derived from the Annual Censuses of Employment figures. The use of the Census information tended to reduce figures.

SOURCE: Occupational Survey of Engineering and Related Industries Great Britain, Department of Employment Gazette, November 1975. p. 116.

Table 12. MINIMUM WAGE RATES FOR APPRENTICES IN SELECTED OECD COUNTRIES

COUNTRY	OCCUPATION	MOST COMMON LENGTH OF TRAINING (YEARS)	RANGE OF MINIMUM APPRENTICE WAGE RATES AS % OF MINIMUM OR PREVAILING RATES FOR SKILLED WORKERS
New Zealand	Engineering	4 – 5	42 – 90
	Engineering	4	48 – 90
	Engineering	3 – 5	42 – 78
Australia			
Queensland	b)	4	40 – 90
Canada			
Alberta	b)	3 – 4	45 – 90
Ontario	b)	3 – 5	40 – 80
Prince Edward Is.	b)	3 – 4	60 – 90
France	All industry	2	25 – 55[a]
	Other	1 – 3	15 – 60[a]
United States	b)	4	40 – 80

NOTES: a) Of the national minimum wage (SMIC) for those under 18, 10% more for those over 18.
b) Many occupations.

SOURCES: National reports.

Table 13. WAGE RATES SET BY COLLECTIVE BARGAINING FOR FIRST AND LAST YEAR APPRENTICES AND STARTING CRAFTWORKERS, GERMANY, 1976-77

OCCUPATION	DURATION OF APPRENTICESHIP (YEARS)	APPRENTICES MONTHLY WAGE RATE (DM) FIRST YEAR	APPRENTICES MONTHLY WAGE RATE (DM) LAST YEAR	STARTING CRAFTWORKERS WAGE RATE MONTHLY (DM)	STARTING CRAFTWORKERS WAGE RATE HOURLY (DM)
1	1	2	3	4	5
Metal	4	377	521	985 – 1,173	7.5
Chemicals	4	412	692	1,473 – 1,578	
Bakeries	3	310	480	..	6.4 – 7.0
Hairdressing	3	170	230	655	
Wholesale trade	3	325	455	1,035	
Retail trade	4	330	550	900	
Private banks	3	475	595	1,423	
Private insurance	3	580	710	1,371	
Public service	3	340	504	1,044 – 1,342	
Engineering technician	3	300	405	1,314 – 1,824	
Dentist assistant	3	315	440	1,085[a]	
Hotel and guest house	3	370	470		5.4 – 7.3
Coal mining	2	640	650		72.6[b]
Ceramics	4	413	538		7.4
Shipping	4	380	530		8.0
Plastics	4	395	490		7.6
Textiles	4	421	575		7.3
Paper	3	354	491		6.7
Printing	4	382	695		8.4
Leather goods	3	325	375		5.0 – 6.1
Wood furniture	3	265	345		6.6 – 7.8
Clothing	3	350	475		7.5 – 8.1
Construction	3	395	698		9.2
Painters	3	253	402		8.6 – 9.6

NOTES: a) Plus 25% for completed apprenticeship.
b) Per shift.

SOURCE: Bundesministerium für Arbeit und Sozialordnung.

OECD SALES AGENTS
DÉPOSITAIRES DES PUBLICATIONS DE L'OCDE

ARGENTINA – ARGENTINE
Carlos Hirsch S.R.L., Florida 165,
BUENOS-AIRES, Tel. 33-1787-2391 Y 30-7122

AUSTRALIA – AUSTRALIE
Australia & New Zealand Book Company Pty Ltd.,
23 Cross Street, (P.O.B. 459)
BROOKVALE NSW 2100 Tel. 938-2244

AUSTRIA – AUTRICHE
Gerold and Co., Graben 31, WIEN 1. Tel. 52.22.35

BELGIUM – BELGIQUE
LCLS
44 rue Otlet, B 1070 BRUXELLES .Tel. 02-521 28 13

BRAZIL – BRÉSIL
Mestre Jou S.A., Rua Guaipà 518,
Caixa Postal 24090, 05089 SAO PAULO 10. Tel. 261-1920
Rua Senador Dantas 19 s/205-6, RIO DE JANEIRO GB.
Tel. 232-07. 32

CANADA
Renouf Publishing Company Limited,
2182 St. Catherine Street West,
MONTREAL, Quebec H3H 1M7 Tel. (514) 937-3519

DENMARK – DANEMARK
Munksgaards Boghandel,
Nørregade 6, 1165 KØBENHAVN K. Tel. (01) 12 85 70

FINLAND – FINLANDE
Akateeminen Kirjakauppa
Keskuskatu 1, 00100 HELSINKI 10. Tel. 625.901

FRANCE
Bureau des Publications de l'OCDE,
2 rue André-Pascal, 75775 PARIS CEDEX 16. Tel. (1) 524.81.67
Principal correspondant :
13602 AIX-EN-PROVENCE : Librairie de l'Université.
Tel. 26.18.08

GERMANY – ALLEMAGNE
Alexander Horn,
D - 6200 WIESBADEN, Spiegelgasse 9
Tel. (6121) 37-42-12

GREECE – GRÈCE
Librairie Kauffmann, 28 rue du Stade,
ATHÈNES 132. Tel. 322.21.60

HONG-KONG
Government Information Services,
Sales and Publications Office, Beaconsfield House, 1st floor,
Queen's Road, Central. Tel. H-233191

ICELAND – ISLANDE
Snaebjörn Jónsson and Co., h.f.,
Hafnarstraeti 4 and 9, P.O.B. 1131, REYKJAVIK.
Tel. 13133/14281/11936

INDIA – INDE
Oxford Book and Stationery Co.:
NEW DELHI, Scindia House. Tel. 45896
CALCUTTA, 17 Park Street. Tel. 240832

ITALY – ITALIE
Libreria Commissionaria Sansoni:
Via Lamarmora 45, 50121 FIRENZE. Tel. 579751
Via Bartolini 29, 20155 MILANO. Tel. 365083
Sub-depositari:
Editrice e Libreria Herder,
Piazza Montecitorio 120, 00 186 ROMA. Tel. 674628
Libreria Hoepli, Via Hoepli 5, 20121 MILANO. Tel. 865446
Libreria Lattes, Via Garibaldi 3, 10122 TORINO. Tel. 519274
La diffusione delle edizioni OCSE è inoltre assicurata dalle migliori
librerie nelle città più importanti.

JAPAN – JAPON
OECD Publications and Information Center
Akasaka Park Building, 2-3-4 Akasaka, Minato-ku,
TOKYO 107. Tel. 586-2016

KOREA - CORÉE
Pan Korea Book Corporation,
P.O.Box n° 101 Kwangwhamun, SÉOUL. Tel. 72-7369

LEBANON – LIBAN
Documenta Scientifica/Redico,
Edison Building, Bliss Street, P.O.Box 5641, BEIRUT.
Tel. 354429–344425

MEXICO & CENTRAL AMERICA
Centro de Publicaciones de Organismos Internacionales S.A.,
Av. Chapultepec 345, Apartado Postal 6-981
MEXICO 6, D.F. Tel. 533-45-09

THE NETHERLANDS – PAYS-BAS
Staatsuitgeverij
Chr. Plantijnstraat
'S-GRAVENHAGE. Tel. 070-814511
Voor bestellingen: Tel. 070-624551

NEW ZEALAND – NOUVELLE-ZÉLANDE
The Publications Manager,
Government Printing Office,
WELLINGTON: Mulgrave Street (Private Bag),
World Trade Centre, Cubacade, Cuba Street,
Rutherford House, Lambton Quay, Tel. 737-320
AUCKLAND: Rutland Street (P.O.Box 5344), Tel. 32.919
CHRISTCHURCH: 130 Oxford Tce (Private Bag), Tel. 50.331
HAMILTON: Barton Street (P.O.Box 857), Tel. 80.103
DUNEDIN: T & G Building, Princes Street (P.O.Box 1104),
Tel. 78.294

NORWAY – NORVÈGE
Johan Grundt Tanums Bokhandel,
Karl Johansgate 41/43, OSLO 1. Tel. 02-332980

PAKISTAN
Mirza Book Agency, 65 Shahrah Quaid-E-Azam, LAHORE 3.
Tel. 66839

PHILIPPINES
R.M. Garcia Publishing House, 903 Quezon Blvd. Ext.,
QUEZON CITY, P.O.Box 1860 – MANILA. Tel. 99.98.47

PORTUGAL
Livraria Portugal, Rua do Carmo 70-74, LISBOA 2. Tel. 360582/3

SPAIN – ESPAGNE
Mundi-Prensa Libros, S.A.
Castelló 37, Apartado 1223, MADRID-1. Tel. 275.46.55
Libreria Bastinos, Pelayo, 52, BARCELONA 1. Tel. 222.06.00

SWEDEN – SUÈDE
AB CE Fritzes Kungl Hovbokhandel,
Box 16 356, S 103 27 STH, Regeringsgatan 12,
DS STOCKHOLM. Tel. 08/23 89 00

SWITZERLAND – SUISSE
Librairie Payot, 6 rue Grenus, 1211 GENÈVE 11. Tel. 022-31.89.50

TAIWAN – FORMOSE
National Book Company,
84-5 Sing Sung Rd., Sec. 3, TAIPEI 107. Tel. 321.0698

UNITED KINGDOM – ROYAUME-UNI
H.M. Stationery Office, P.O.B. 569,
LONDON SE1 9 NH. Tel. 01-928-6977, Ext. 410 or
49 High Holborn, LONDON WC1V 6 HB (personal callers)
Branches at: EDINBURGH, BIRMINGHAM, BRISTOL,
MANCHESTER, CARDIFF, BELFAST.

UNITED STATES OF AMERICA
OECD Publications and Information Center, Suite 1207,
1750 Pennsylvania Ave., N.W. WASHINGTON, D.C. 20006.
Tel. (202)724-1857

VENEZUELA
Libreria del Este, Avda. F. Miranda 52, Edificio Galipàn,
CARACAS 106. Tel. 32 23 01/33 26 04/33 24 73

YUGOSLAVIA – YOUGOSLAVIE
Jugoslovenska Knjiga, Terazije 27, P.O.B. 36, BEOGRAD.
Tel. 621-992

Les commandes provenant de pays où l'OCDE n'a pas encore désigné de dépositaire peuvent être adressées à :
OCDE, Bureau des Publications, 2 rue André-Pascal, 75775 PARIS CEDEX 16.
Orders and inquiries from countries where sales agents have not yet been appointed may be sent to:
OECD, Publications Office, 2 rue André-Pascal, 75775 PARIS CEDEX 16.

OECD PUBLICATIONS, 2, rue André-Pascal, 75775 Paris Cedex 16 - No. 40.897 1978

PRINTED IN FRANCE